All New Fire HD 6 & HD 7 User Guide – Newbie to Expert in 2 Hours!

by Tom Edwards and Jenna Edwards

All New Fire HD 6 & HD 7 User Guide

– Newbie to Expert in 2 Hours!

by Tom Edwards & Jenna Edwards

Other Books By Tom & Jenna Edwards

250+ Best Kindle Fire HDX and HD Apps for the New Kindle Fire Owner

Kindle Fire HDX User Guide – Newbie to Expert in 2 Hours!

Chromecast User Guide – Newbie to Expert in 1 Hour!

Amazon Fire TV User Guide — Newbie to Expert in 1 Hour!

Apple TV User Guide — Newbie to Expert in 1 Hour!

Want the Latest Kindle Fire HD App News?

Before we start, I just want to let you know about the **FREE updates** we offer all our customers. As you may know we are also the authors of **250+ Best Kindle Fire HDX and HD Apps** and we send out a monthly email with tips, tricks, news and reviews of five top apps for you to consider. These apps will help you get the best from your Kindle Fire, so if you want to take advantage of our monthly recommendations then …

Sign up for the updates here: www.Lyntons.com/updates

Don't worry; we hate spam as much as you do so we will never share your details with anyone.

Contents

Introduction

When we first published our Kindle Fire App review guide – **250+ Best Kindle Fire Apps for the New Kindle Fire Owner** – we added in a small bonus section which included a few tips and tricks for the new Kindle Fire user. We soon started receiving emails from customers asking for more of the same, so we published the Kindle Fire User Guide. When Amazon released its Kindle Fire HD 2nd Generation model in September 2013, we followed suit and updated the Guide to reflect its many upgrades. In September 2014 Amazon upgraded the Kindle Fire HD 7" to the new Fire HD 6 and HD 7. So here it is, our complete and comprehensive, easy to understand guide to getting the most from your new Fire HD tablet computer!

We've taken everything we know, scoured the official online Amazon guides, then read a whole lot more and put it all together for you here. What you are reading now is a user guide for both beginners and the tech savvy. This book contains the basics you need to navigate easily around your device but also the more advanced tips and tricks that will have you using your Kindle like a pro before you know it.

Before we get started we *highly recommend* that you download and install Kindle for PC (**www.amazon.com/gp/kindle/pc**) or Kindle for Mac (**www.amazon.com/gp/kindle/mac**). Doing so will allow you to consult this user guide on your desktop device whilst at the same time exploring the new features of your Kindle Fire tablet.

So let's get started right at the beginning… what is the Fire HD?

When the original Kindle device was released, it was designed purely as an ebook reader. The new Fire HD tablet however is so much more than just an ebook reader – having said that though, we still use it for reading lots of books.

The new Fire HD 6 and HD 7 tablets are the latest generation of tablet offerings from Amazon. The first Kindle Fire HD was released in September 2012, only one year after the standard-display Fire tablet's debut. The first Kindle Fire HD caused a big stir in the tablet market with its improved color screen resolution and extremely competitive pricing compared to other tablets such as Apple's iPad. The 2013 release of the 7" Kindle Fire HD brought even more improvements, including faster performance and a simplified user interface. The 2014 upgrade produced the Fire HD, available in 6" or 7" screen size, with even faster performance and a rear and front facing camera for live video chat and self-portraits.

Whether you are already a Fire HD owner, or just thinking of buying one, this book will guide you through the basics of setting it up, using it, and getting the most out of all the features this great device has to offer.

Just What is a Tablet?

It's a mobile computer operated by touchscreen that stores information on the Internet. This approach to data storage, called "the cloud," eliminates the need for an internal hard drive.

Tablets fill the gap between smartphones and laptops. A tablet has all of the functions of a smartphone and more, but the display size is three to four times as big. Navigating a tablet's touchscreen is similar to using a smartphone, which eliminates the need for a keyboard. Just like a smartphone, tablets can access the Internet and use applications ("apps") to make all kinds of online tasks easier, from checking the weather to balancing your checkbook to shopping at online stores like Amazon. The tablet's cloud-based storage cuts down on the weight and bulk so familiar to laptop owners. For many users, it offers the best of both worlds.

Although the price makes the new Fire HD 6 and HD 7 tablets very attractive, the real selling point is the way they integrate effortlessly with Amazon's enormous online store. From its humble beginnings as an online bookstore, this ecommerce giant has grown into the world's largest retailer, and Amazon's digital content offerings have been a real success story too. From your Fire HD you can choose from over 23 million media items, including books, movies, TV shows, apps and games, audiobooks, and music files. It's like holding the biggest library on the planet in the palm of your hand.

The new Fire HD 6 and HD 7 tablets come standard with a 1280x800 HD color display. The HD 7 has a 216ppi 7" display with 22" of viewable area, while the HD 6 has a 252ppi 6" display with 16" of viewable area. Both tablets offer Dolby audio, with dual stereo speakers on the HD 7 and one mono speaker on the HD 6. Both tablets feature your choice of 8GB or 16GB of internal storage, single-band Wi-Fi access to the Internet, a quad-core processor with speeds up to 1.5GHz, and free unlimited cloud storage for your Amazon content.

Amazon made three very nice additions to the new Fire HD 6 and HD 7. The first is a front-facing VGA camera and a 2 MP rear-facing camera. A built in microphone is now a standard feature, and both tablets are now available in your choice of colors: black, white, magenta, citron, or cobalt. Also standard are a headphone jack, Bluetooth capability, and a port for a micro USB cable.

If you want a 4G wireless connection, you should purchase the new Fire HDX models because 4G is not available on the new Fire HD 6 and HD 7.

One of our favorite things about the new Fire HD 6 and HD 7 is that they are Android-based tablets. Why is this so great? Because the Fire HD will run hundreds of free Android apps that you can download in the Amazon Store, along with hundreds more third-party apps. It's true that the Android operating system has been altered by Amazon into a proprietary firmware for the Fire HD, so it won't run all of the Android apps in the Google Play app store. However, Amazon has built the device with a menu option to allow sideloading of non-Amazon apps, and we have been very satisfied with the results.

Please don't panic if, at this stage, all this tech jargon is a like a foreign language to you – by the end of this book you'll not think twice about using terms like "sideloading" and "apps." **We wrote this book for complete beginners as well as Fire HD veterans**. Our aim is not only to cover the how-to basics, but also to show you some of the lesser-known features of the Fire HD that really make it fun to own.

The new Fire HD 6 and HD 7 tablets are amazing devices with a wealth of capabilities and a nearly unlimited supply of fresh content to experience, with more being added every day to the Amazon store. We hope to show you why these tablets are the ultimate media device for getting more enjoyment out of life in our digital world.

1. Getting Started

Controls and Battery

The power switch is located on the top edge of the new Kindle HD 6 and HD 7 when you hold it in the "portrait" position, with the long edges in each hand and the short edges at the top and bottom. In the "landscape" position, with the long edges at the top and bottom, the switch is on the rightside when the touchscreen is facing you. Thanks to the auto-rotate feature, your device will display correctly in any position shortly after you power it up.

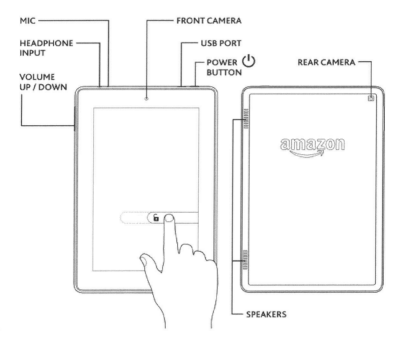

To turn on your device, press & hold the power button for 2–3 seconds.

To put it to sleep while the power is on, press and release the power button again.

To wake up the device, press and release the power button again.

Then touch the lock button on the touchscreen and slide your finger from right to left.

To turn it off, press and hold the power button and follow the prompt to either shut down or cancel.

You will need battery power to operate your Fire HD, so it's best to start charging it up as soon as you take it out of its box for the first time. A micro-USB 2.0 cable and a 5W USB adapter are included in the box. Plug the full-size end of the cable into the adapter and plug the adapter into the wall. Plug the micro end of the cable into your Fire HD's micro-USB port located just to the left of the power button. (You can also charge the battery from a USB 2.0 port of your desktop or laptop computer, or a USB hub, but it will take longer than using the Fire HD adapter.)

The Fire HD's battery is claimed to last about 8 hours on full charge, and we have found this to be accurate, unless we're doing a lot of downloads or other power-hungry tasks. Charging a completely dead battery through the USB adapter takes about 4 hours.

The Fire HD 6 and HD 7 are designed for you to hold it in either portrait or landscape orientation, which gives you great flexibility in adapting the device to the tasks you're using it for. Even better, it changes orientation automatically along with you when you rotate it 90 degrees. You can even use it upside down!

The Fire HD uses a touchscreen, so you will be navigating through the menus with your fingertips. There are two touch commands you will be using often, so take a moment to practice them on the touchscreen. Tapping means quickly touching your fingertip to an image on the screen, similar to clicking a mouse, and lifting it. You will tap once to select an item, such as a button, app icon, or block of text, and you will double tap to open an item. Swiping means sweeping your finger across the screen. You will swipe to scroll, to turn a page, or to open menus.

When you turn on your Fire HD 6 or HD 7 for the first time, it will automatically take you to an introductory demo screen that starts the registration process for the device. This screen will keep appearing until you register.

Setup and Registration

Your Fire HD relies heavily on Amazon's cloud server, so your new device won't do much until you register it and link it with your Amazon user account. Registering allows you to wirelessly download your apps, books, music, movies, photos, documents, and other data that make your Fire HD so much fun. Most new Fire HD owners will already have an Amazon account that they used to purchase their device, but if you received your tablet as a gift and don't have an account, you can set one up during the registration steps.

First, turn on your Fire HD 6 or HD 7 and slide the lock button from right to left to unlock it. When the registration screen appears, choose your language and tap *Continue*.

Next you will see a list of networks for connecting to the Internet. Your Kindle automatically scans for available wireless networks within range and lists them. Tap the network you want to use. Networks that require a password will have a lock symbol next to them, and you will need to know the password for that network (not your Amazon account password).

If a wireless network password is required, the Fire HD's built-in onscreen keyboard will pop up so you can fill in the password box. The Shift key on the keyboard is labeled with an upward arrow ⇧ and lets you type capital letters. The **?123** key switches the keyboard layout between letters or numbers and symbols. When you tap this key, it will change the keyboard to numbers and symbols; tap it again to bring back the regular keyboard with letters.

When you have chosen a network, tap the *Connect* button. This network is now stored in your Fire HD, which will automatically find it and reconnect whenever it detects the signal.

Now that you are connected to the Internet, a 'Register Your Fire Tablet' screen will appear. If you already have an Amazon account, type in the email address and password that you normally use to log in to the account. If you don't have an Amazon account, tap the *Create Account* key to set up a new login and password with Amazon using the built-in keyboard.

Tap the *Register* key and select a time zone if your Fire HD asks you to. If you see a Deregister button where the Register button should appear, you probably received your Fire HD as a gift. Simply tap *Deregister* and go through the registration process above, using your own Amazon account information.

Tap *Confirm* to finish registering your Fire HD. You will be prompted to purchase a 30-day free trial of Amazon Prime with the Get Started button. If you want to skip this step for now, tap the *No Thanks* link to continue.

Next you will be prompted to link your Facebook, Goodreads and Twitter accounts with your Fire HD. You can do this now by clicking on the Facebook, Goodreads or Twitter links, entering your login and password for the social network, and tapping *Connect*. You can also skip this step for now by tapping *Next*.

After registration, your Fire HD will run you through a very short tutorial about your device. Tap *Get Started*, follow the prompts to move quickly through the tutorial, and tap *Finish* to end it.

You will now see your "Home" screen!

Navigation

The starting point for all of your navigation on your Fire HD is the Home screen. If you ever get lost while navigating your Fire Tablet, simply tap the center of the screen, look for the little house icon to appear in the middle of the bottom toolbar, and tap it to go back to Home.

Here is a detailed anatomy of the Home screen from top to bottom, and how to find your way around it.

Status Bar: The Status Bar is always visible at the very top of the screen and gives you information about your Fire HD device. From left to right, its functions are:

② **Notifications:** messages sent to you by applications and games

◀ **Location-based services indicator:** lets you know whether the Kindle is keeping track of your location

Wi-Fi indicator: tells you how strong your Wi-Fi signal is

 Battery indicator: displays how much battery power you have left

5:03 **Clock:** displays your local time

Navigation Bar: This black bar with white lettering runs across the top of your Fire HD Home screen. It's the gateway to the enormous world of content that awaits you as a Kindle user. Its two main functions are the Search box, and the Content Libraries.

Search Box: Tap the magnifying glass icon in the Navigation Bar to bring up the Search Box. Wait for the onscreen keyboard to appear and then type whatever you're looking for into this box to search the web, Amazon Stores, or My Stuff containing stored Fire HD materials. The onscreen keyboard pops up automatically for any task that requires text input. (We'll show you how to use the onscreen keyboard feature in more detail in **Chapter 2**).

Content Libraries: These sections of the Navigation Bar divide your stored Fire HD materials into categories to make everything easier to find. Tap once on a category to display its contents and select an item. From left to right, the libraries are Shop, Games, Apps, Books, Music, Videos, Newsstand (for magazines and newspapers), Audiobooks, Web, Photos, Docs (documents), and Offers. To access the hidden libraries, just swipe to scroll the Navigation Bar menu across from right to left, or rotate your Fire tablet to the landscape position.

When you open any Content Library, you will find that it has its own sidebar menu featuring a wealth of sort options, categories, and settings. The sidebar menu displays when you either swipe from left to right, or tap the menu icon with the three horizontal lines in the far upper left corner of the library next to its name. Swipe right to left to hide the sidebar menu. Your Kindle's Email, Calendar, and Contacts apps also have sidebar menus with the same navigation as the libraries.

Carousel: This colorful display occupies the top half of the Home screen under the Navigation Bar. It shows graphic icons for all of the content you have viewed recently, whether it's a book, app, song, movie, or other library item. The most recently viewed item will appear first, then the next most recently viewed, and so on. If you haven't finished reading a book, the cover image in the Carousel will display a bookmark badge showing how much of it you have already read.

Navigating the Carousel is easy. To scroll the display of content icons, swipe your finger across it. To open an item, tap it. To select an item, press and hold it. If you want to delete an item from the Carousel, tap and hold it until a white menu bar appears at the top of the screen with a Remove option; then tap *Remove*. Deleting an item from the Carousel only removes it from the screen, not from your Fire HD or your Amazon Cloud Library. To remove the item from your device, tap *More* on the white menu bar and tap *Delete from Device*. The item will remain stored in your Amazon Cloud Library, ready for you to download it to your Fire HD again at any time. Tap the Home icon or the black arrow on the left side of the white menu to return to your Home screen.

Customers Also Bought: This is Amazon's well-known cross-selling feature that suggests content for you based on items in your library that are similar to those purchased by others. It appears just under your Carousel (in portrait mode only) and can be a convenient shopping feature (in addition to a smart marketing technique by Amazon!). Tap any item to see its details in the Amazon store.

You can remove this display from your home page if you like, using the Quick Actions menu. (Other features of this menu are explained in **Chapter 2**). Swipe down from the top of the screen to display the menu; then choose *Settings* by tapping it. Next, tap *Applications*; then tap *Home Screen*. Finally, tap *Hide*.

Options Bar: The Options Bar changes its appearance in the Fire HD Home screen depending on which content or applications you're using. When you open a content library, the Options Bar will appear as a narrow strip of icons across the bottom of the Home screen. When no libraries are open, or when you're viewing a piece of content such as an ebook, it disappears, and you will need to tap the center of the screen to open it.

The icons on the Options Bar will vary, depending on which content library you're using, but the choices are pretty intuitive. There are also several standard options that always appear on the Options Bar when you make it visible. Here is a brief description of each standard option from left to right.

Back: Tap the arrow pointing to the left to go back to the previous screen you were using, just as if you were using a web browser.

Home: Tap the house icon to go back to the Home screen.

Search: Tap the magnifying glass icon to bring up a search box identical to the one that appears on the Home screen under the Status Bar.

Close Onscreen Keyboard: if a keyboard icon appears in place of the Back arrow, tap it if you want to hide the onscreen keyboard.

QuickSwitch: The lower one-third of your Home screen displays an icon for each of your recently opened content items, allowing you to quickly move back and forth between different types of content without using the Navigation Bar. The QuickSwitch menu is also available from the Home Screen or Options Bar by swiping upward from the bottom edge of your screen, allowing you to quickly switch between the Carousel and grid view for recent items.

You can also access QuickSwitch when you have a piece of content open in full screen mode by swiping upward from the bottom of your screen.

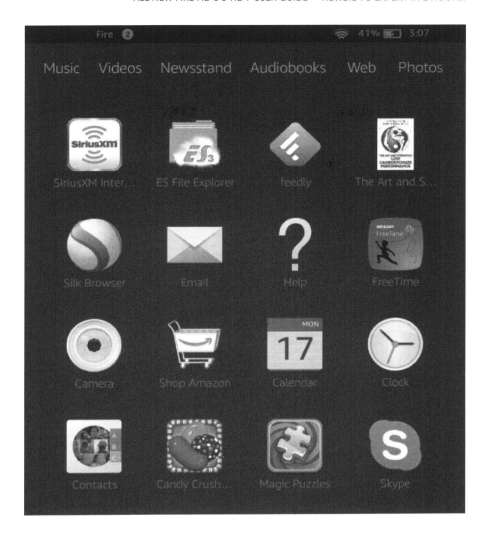

Quick Actions Menu: This menu is hidden on your Home screen until you swipe down from the top edge of the screen to make it visible. From here you can adjust items such as clock, speaker volume, screen brightness, security features, wireless connections, and synchronize your Kindle device with your cloud storage account on Amazon. One very important function on this menu that you should take care of right away is setting a password for your lock screen (see instructions in **Chapter 2**).

We will explore the tasks available in the Quick Actions Menu in depth in **Chapter 2**.

Cloud Collections

The Cloud Collections feature offers a number of sophisticated sorting options for all of the media in your Amazon Cloud Library, including favorites and categories that you can create your own names for. The point of this feature is to give you the opportunity to group certain items in a certain place so that you can access them more easily for example you might want to create a category especially for children's games so that they are all together in one place. A collection can include games, apps, books, audiobooks, and documents. You can't add music, videos, newsstand items, or photos to a Cloud Collection. Cloud Collections will sync your Kindle Content Libraries across all of your devices and apps that can access Amazon's cloud.

To create a collection, in the Navigation Bar tap *Apps, Books*, or *Docs*, swipe left to display the sidebar menu, and tap *Collections*. You will see a list of collections you already created and a + symbol for adding a new collection. Tap it, give the collection a name, and scroll down the menu to check off the items you want to add you your collection. You can also tap and hold any item in the carousel, tap the *More* icon, and tap *Create a Collection*.

To access any collection, tap *Apps, Books*, or *Docs* in the navigation bar, swipe left, tap Collections, and tap the collection you want to access. To add to a collection, tap and hold any eligible item, tap the *More* icon, and check the box next to each collection you want to add the item to. You can edit a collection by tapping it in the sidebar of the Apps, Books, or Docs library on the Navigation Bar. To change its title, tap it and type in your new title. To remove an item, press and hold it, then drag it outside of the collection. Delete a collection by pressing and holding it, then tapping *Delete Collection*. Deleting a collection from your Fire HD deletes the collection from all of your devices that can access it, but does not delete any of the items in the collection from your Amazon Cloud Library.

Import a collection: With Cloud Collections, collections are automatically stored in the Cloud and can be synced between Kindle Paperwhite, Kindle Fire HD (2nd Generation), Kindle Fire HDX, Kindle for iPad, iPhone, and iPod touch, and Kindle for Android.

Content Storage and Access

The Fire HD 6 and HD 7 have some built-in data storage, either 8GB or 16GB options available for both devices. When you purchase and download content, such as a book, video, or app, from the Amazon store, it is stored on your Fire tablet as long there's enough space on its internal storage drive. Keep in mind that some of your tablet's storage space is taken up by its operating software, so not all of it will be available for storing your data.

Amazon Cloud Library: If you're new to the world of tablets, you might be confused by all the talk you've been hearing about "the cloud." Because they have much less internal data storage than a laptop or desktop computer, tablets use one or more online data storage space companies to store large quantities of data. These companies are collectively called "the cloud." Some tablets also pull all or part of their internal functioning from the cloud, as is the case with the Silk browser on your Fire HD.

Amazon is an online data storage company, and it calls its cloud storage product Amazon Cloud Drive. Anyone who has ever purchased digital content from their store gets their own free Cloud Library on Amazon's Cloud Drive for their music, movies, apps, or ebooks.

If you accidentally delete one of these files from your computer or tablet, simply open a browser window, go to your Amazon account, choose Digital Content from the menu, and download the file again. Space in your Amazon Cloud Library for Amazon content is free and unlimited – it grows as you purchase more digital stuff from Amazon.

Your fire HD tablet is designed to automatically sync with your Amazon Cloud Library. Each of your Content Libraries in the Navigation Bar has a set of options on the right side of its top toolbar for managing your cloud data. The Store button on the far right toggles back and forth between the Amazon store and the Content Library for that category.

To the left of the Store button you will see a pair of tabs: one marked Cloud, and one marked Device. When you tap the Cloud tab, you will see a list of all of your Amazon media purchases for that library, and you can download any of them to your Fire HD, where they will show up when you switch to the Device tab. Purchases you have already downloaded to your device have a checkmark on their icon in their Content Library.

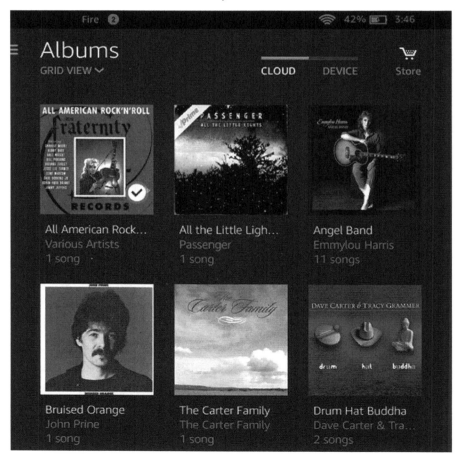

To view all of your Amazon digital content purchases at once in your Amazon Cloud Library, open the Silk browser from the Carousel or QuickSwitch menu and go to the Amazon home page. Look for your name in the upper right corner, click the small black triangle next to Your Account, and choose Manage Your Content and Devices from the drop-down menu.

Storing Your Digital Content: As well as storing digital content you bought on Amazon, you can also use your Amazon Cloud Library to store pre-existing digital content that you already own, such as your personal photos, MP3's, home videos, etc. See **Chapter 8** for more info on how to use the Cloud Drive Desktop Application.

All Amazon customers get free unlimited storage for their Amazon digital content purchases and photos taken with Fire devices. In addition you get 5GB of free Cloud Drive storage, plus room for 250 MP3 music files in your Amazon Music account. Your content purchases from Amazon are stored in your Cloud Library for free, so they don't count against your free Cloud Drive quota. Amazon encourages you to upload your photos and music collection to its Cloud Drive service. Your free 5GB of storage will hold about 5,000 photos, while your free Amazon Music account holds 250 songs. After you use up your free storage, you can purchase more from Amazon Cloud Drive for a very reasonable annual subscription fee.

Use your existing amazon.com account.

Your Amazon.com email:

Password:

Sign In

By signing in you agree to the Cloud Drive Terms of Use

New to Amazon.com?

Forgot your password?

Conditions of Use   Privacy Notice
© 1996-2014, Amazon.com, Inc. or its affiliates

2. Customizing Your Settings

Our instructions in this chapter will show you how to configure some of the lesser-known settings on your Fire HD to match how you use your device. The Fire HD's user settings allow you some pretty nice customization options. Although you won't be changing them often, they make your navigation experience much faster and less frustrating. The Fire tablet is small enough to go wherever you go, so we encourage you to make your display uniquely you!

Quick Actions Menu

Nearly all user settings are changed from the Quick Actions Menu. This menu is hidden on the Fire HD until you swipe down from the top edge of the screen to make it visible. To hide it again, swipe upward toward the top edge of the screen. You can adjust items such as screen brightness and, security features, wireless connections, and synchronize your Fire HD device with your Cloud Library on Amazon or access the Help menu. To return to the Home screen at any time, tap the *Home* icon on the Options Bar in the bottom center of your Fire HD screen.

Here are the six major Quick Actions Menu items, from left to right. Some of these menu items have sub-menus. To go up one level from within any sub-menu, tap the *left arrow* to the left of sub-menu name.

 Auto-Rotate: Tap this basic on/off key to control your Fire tablet's automatic screen rotation. Off locks your device in its current orientation, either portrait or landscape. On allows you to easily switch your tablet's orientation by tilting it.

 Brightness: Tap to adjust screen brightness on your Fire HD.

Wireless: Tap to turn wireless access on or off, connect to a Wi-Fi network, control a Bluetooth device, connect to a VPN private network, or control Location-Based Services.

Turn wireless access on or off: This first item on the Fire HD's Wireless menu is labeled Airplane Mode, but it's good for a lot more than air travel. We turn off our wireless connection whenever we're not using it to save the Fire HD's battery life. Tap *On* to activate Airplane Mode and turn off wireless access. You'll see an airplane icon in the Fire HD's status bar until you tap *Off* to reactivate wireless access.

Wi-Fi: If your Fire HD doesn't automatically detect a wireless network you want to join, you can add it manually. First, make sure Airplane Mode is off so your tablet can receive wireless signals. Tap *Wi-Fi*, then tap *Join Other Network*. The onscreen keyboard will pop up so you can enter the network name. Next tap the security type if the network is secure, and the password if the network requires one. Tap *Save*, and then tap *Connect*. If you want to keep your Fire HD from connecting to a stored network automatically, tap *Wi-Fi*, tap the name of the network, and tap *Forget*.

Bluetooth: The Fire HD 6 and HD 7 supports some wireless Bluetooth devices, including an external keyboard, mouse, speakers, or headset. It does not support Bluetooth microphones or headsets with a built-in microphone. See **Chapter 10** for pairing your Kindle with an external Bluetooth device.

VPN: This menu will allow you to connect to a virtual private network (VPN) if you have access to one. To add a VPN, tap the + icon at the top right of the screen and enter your login information for the network.

Location-Based Services: This function uses Wi-Fi to tell your Fire HD your location for use with apps that display localized data, such as mapping, weather, and traffic. The default setting is Off. Tap *On* to activate it, and you will see a small triangle icon appear in the Status Bar at the top of your screen, next to the wireless indicator, to show that the Fire HD is tracking your location. Below the on/off control you can customize which applications you allow to access your location. Note that this function will make you charge your battery more often.

 Quiet Time: You can use this basic on/off key to set your Fire HD to give you Quiet Time by disabling all notifications.

 Help: We like to use this menu to get quick access to Amazon's online Fire tablet User Guide. There is also a wireless connection, Bluetooth, troubleshooting section, and an Amazon customer service contact option that includes email, chat, and telephone support as well as a feedback form.

Settings: Tap to access a long (very long!) list of additional settings for your Fire HD. To make things less confusing for you, we cover this menu in a separate section below.

The Settings Menu

The Settings menu at the far right of the Quick Actions menu offers you extra options that you may want to adjust to suit how you use your Fire HD, including things like customizing the Keyboard function and setting up Parental Controls. Here is a detailed explanation of each item on the Settings menu, as they appear from top to bottom on your Fire tablet.

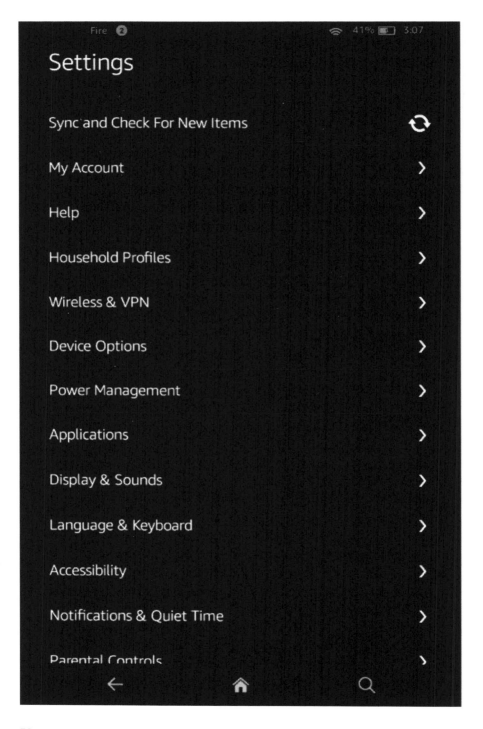

Sync and Check For New Items: Amazon automatically syncs your digital content across all of the devices you register with them, such as your laptop or desktop computer, along with your Fire HD. To manually sync your Fire HD, tap this menu item to connect to Amazon's Cloud Library and make sure the Amazon books, movies, music, and other data on your device's storage drive are up to date.

My Account: This sub menu controls how your Fire HD talks to your Amazon account. The e-mail address you see under this option is a unique Amazon account e-mail that is assigned to you when you register your Fire HD. If you want to deregister your device so you can sell it or give it away, tap the *Deregister* button. (To erase all content from your Fire HD's storage drive, refer to the Device menu below.) You can also change your Amazon account settings from this menu and manage how your Fire tablet connects with Facebook, Goodreads, and Twitter, if you skipped this step when you registered.

Help: This is the same sub menu that appears when you tap *Help* directly from the Quick Actions menu (see above).

Household Profiles: This sub menu lets you register additional user profiles on your Fire HD, each with its own carousel, collections, preferences, apps, and content. One additional adult user may create a profile on your Fire HD by clicking *Add Adult* and either providing or creating an Amazon account user name and password. Profiles for up to four children can be added without their own Amazon account. Click *Add Child Profile* and fill in the child's registration information. Amazon recommends that you register kids 8 years old and younger as Amazon FreeTime users (see **Chapter 4**), but the choice is yours.

To switch profiles, lock your Fire HD by pressing the power button, then press the power button again to display the lock screen. Tap your profile icon in the upper left corner of the screen, and then select the profile you want to use. To switch from a child profile to an adult profile, you will need to enter your lock screen PIN.

Wireless & VPN: This sub menu duplicates the Wireless settings option on the Quick Actions Menu (see above).

Device Options: This sub menu lets you monitor your Fire tablet's battery charge level, see if its firmware version is up to date, change your device name, find your tablet remotely, manage your backup and restore options, change your time zone, check how much memory is available, and check your tablet serial number.

The last option on the Device menu is Reset to Factory Defaults. This item wipes your Fire HD's hard drive completely clean in case you want to sell or give away the device – or if you forget your password and have to reset it (see **Chapter 9**). Treat this menu option with all due respect!

Power Management: This sub menu lets you schedule standby, wireless, and display options to maximize battery life.

Applications: This sub menu lets you manage your apps and see which ones are running. From here you can change an app's notification settings, delete old data that an app has stored on your Fire HD hard drive to free up memory space, and change the way an app interacts with your other content libraries. You can also get rid of the Customers Also Bought display by selecting the Home Recommendations sub menu and tapping *Hide*.

One really important setting in the Applications sub menu is Apps from Unknown Sources. If you want to "sideload" apps that aren't available in the Amazon store, you need to tap *On* for this option. (See **Chapter 4** for more information on sideloading.)

Display & Sounds: Here you can fine-tune how your Fire HD sounds and looks. Sound adjustments include a volume slider or you can use the pair of switches on the right edge of your tablet's case toward the top. This menu also allows you to change your screen brightness, increase or decrease the font size, and adjust the timeout period before the screen goes into lock mode if you don't touch it.

Language & Keyboard Keyboards: Here you can customize the Fire HD onscreen keyboard with some limited word processing functions. You can turn automatic capitalization and autocorrection on or off, and you can choose whether to show suggested corrections and highlight possible misspellings. You can also turn on the keypress sound to get the effect of a mechanical keyboard. We both use this feature even though we feel a bit silly about it – it seems to help with the accuracy of our typing. Kids who grow up using only a touchscreen will wonder why this option even exists! The Keyboards menu also allows you to set languages and keyboard shortcuts for a Bluetooth keyboard if you have one.

Accessibility: This sub menu allows you to adjust your Fire HD for enhanced vision and hearing capabilities. The new Fire HD 6 and HD 7 can be set to provide spoken feedback when you touch the screen, along with closed captioning and screen magnification. These features are especially useful for people with disabilities.

Notifications & Quiet Time: This sub menu allows you to set which apps you want to receive notifications from – for example, setting whether you want your Calendar app to put a notification in your status bar to remind you of an appointment. There are also settings for notifications, such as e-mail alerts, where you can select different alert sounds for different notifications. The Quiet Time sub menu is identical to the one you can access directly from the Quick Actions menu.

Parental Controls: If you want to restrict what other users can see on your Fire tablet (and if, like us, you have kids who love the Fire HD as much as you do, then the answer is going to be yes!), turn on Parental Controls by tapping *On*. You will be prompted to enter a password. (It should be different from the one you use for the lock screen of your Fire HD, and one that your kids are unlikely to guess!) Confirm and tap *Finish*. Important: be sure to write down your password and store it in a safe place. (See **Chapter 9** for what to do if you lose your password.)

Setting your parental controls password brings up a menu where you can give children and anyone else who doesn't have the password the ability to use only the Fire HD features you want them to use. You can use this menu to lock them out of the following functions:

1. Web browser

2. Apps for email, calendars, and contacts

3. Purchasing from the Amazon Store and the app for Amazon Shop

4. Amazon Instant Video

5. Specific Library items, such as books, music, video, or apps

6. Wi-Fi network access

7. Social network access

8. Location-based services

If you want to change any of these Parental Controls later on, or change your password, you will need to reenter your password to unlock this menu.

The Parental Controls menu also lets you manage any child profiles you registered earlier under Household Profiles. Parents should also check out **Chapter 4** for information about Amazon's Free Time app and content delivery program for kids.

Security & Privacy: Here is where you set a password for your lock screen. This is very important because your Fire HD is hooked up to your Amazon account and one-click purchasing. From the Security menu, tap *On*. Enter a password that you can remember easily, but that won't be obvious to an unfriendly person. Confirm and tap *Finish*. When your tablet powers up or goes into timeout, swipe the lock icon and enter your password to unlock it.

Important: be sure to write down your password and store it in a safe place. (See **Chapter 9** for what to do if you lose your password.)

Legal & Compliance: This sub menu has no user commands.

About Special Offers and Screensaver Advertising

Part of the buzz when the first Kindle Fire HD was released concerned Amazon advertising. For a discount ($15 in late 2014), you can buy a Fire HD that displays advertising. (Or, put another way, for an extra fee you can buy a Fire HD with no ads.) We don't mind the ads. At least for now, they're unobtrusive, and if Amazon gets more aggressive about displaying them on our tablet in the future, there's always the option of paying the fee to remove them later on.

Currently, the advertising appears in two places: on the lock screen when the device is locked or in Sleep Mode, and in the "Offers" content library at the far right of the Navigation Bar. If you want to take a closer look at what Amazon is promoting, tap the *Offers* tab.

To unsubscribe from Special Offers, you will need to go to the Amazon store from either the Fire HD Silk browser, or from the browser of your desktop computer. Log in to your Amazon account and go to the *Manage Your Content and Devices page*. Click the center tab labeled *Devices*. The devices you've registered with Amazon will appear across this page. Click your Fire HD device icon and look for *Special Offers*. Your device should say Subscribed. Click *Edit*, and a window will pop up displaying the price to unsubscribe. From here it's just like making any other Amazon purchase. (Note that the Shop Amazon app on your Fire HD won't work for this process.)

Using the Fire HD Keyboard

One of the more interesting aspects of tablet technology is the fact that – mainly because of the limited space the screen affords – the onscreen keyboards are not fixed, but are dynamic, with the ability to change format depending on what you are typing. This means that the keyboard can do things like switch from letters to numbers and symbols (to do this on the Fire HD keyboard tap the **?123** key), or offer the user the new fluid typing technology such as Swyping (see below). The keyboard interface is fairly self-explanatory for anyone who is familiar with the traditional Qwerty keyboard, but here are a couple of short cuts that may prove useful. Please note that if you prefer to use the Swype mode then there are a bunch of different shortcut commands that we go through below.

Delete: delete the character before the cursor by tapping the *delete* key, which is the back arrow with the "**x**" inside in the lower right corner of the onscreen keyboard. To delete all, hold down the *delete* key.

Change keyboard language: Tap and hold the space button to choose from a variety of different languages, including French, Spanish and Japanese.

Hidden capitals lock: Double tap or tap and hold the *Shift* key to keep letters in capital form. Tap *Shift* again at the end when you want to unlock this function.

Quick access to numbers and symbols: When the keyboard is in letters format you will see small numbers or symbols in the corner of each letter button. Tap and hold on the letter key for a second and you will see a white button with the number or symbol. Lift your finger off the letter button and that number or symbol will automatically be inserted into your text.

Top Tip!

If you tap and hold any keyboard button for longer than a second, you can access a grey option box with the different letters, numbers or symbols attributed to that key – simply tap on the option you want to insert it into your text.

Quick new sentence: Double tap the space bar at the end of a sentence to get a period followed by a single space and capitalization of the next word.

Dot com button: When you're using the Silk browser, or email, and you type in a web or email address, a ".com" button appears on the keyboard next to the period button, and if you tap and hold on this button other domain name extensions appear (".org", ".net", etc).

Voice commands: The new Fire HD 6 and HD 7 tablets feature voice commands for entering keyboard characters in the search box. Tap the microphone icon next to the space bar when using any app on your device and tap *Tap to Speak*. Say the words you want to fill in on the search box and watch them appear in the search box. Tap *Tap to Pause* to pause the microphone.

Advanced symbols: When the keyboard is in numbers and symbols format, the shift button changes to a ~\< key – tap on this to access less usual symbols such as foreign currency symbols, square brackets, percentage mark etc.

Editing shortcut: Tap on an empty area near your text to access an Edit tool (which looks like an arrow tab). Tap on this tool and drag it to the place in the text that you want to edit, then lift your finger to release the tool and edit the section. When you're done, tap the edited section again to see the Edit tool – drag to the end of your text and release it to exit the function.

Cut, copy and paste: Tap and hold on a word to access and choose cut, copy or paste options – select more words by sliding the highlight arrows. To paste your copied or cut text, tap and hold on the screen in the place you want to add the text and then choose the paste option.

Using Swype with the Fire HD Keyboard

We never quite mastered the art of two-fingered typing, but we do like Swype. This third-party software program comes pre-loaded on all firmware updates for the new Fire HD 6 and HD 7 tablets and offers all kinds of shortcuts to make using the onscreen keyboard more efficient. Swype isn't an app, so you don't have to do anything special to use it. It does have a learning curve, but the developers claim that users can reach speeds of over 50 words per minute. (We're still working on that!)

You "Swype" a word by tracing a line with your finger across the letter keys in that word. The critical step is lifting your finger when you reach the last letter of the word. You don't have to lift your finger and skip over the letters you don't want in the middle of the word – Swype does that for you by detecting all the possible words that could be formed from the line you traced and listing them across the top of the keyboard display. Touch the right word and Swype will insert it into your text. It also automatically enters spaces between words, provided you lift your finger off the keyboard between swypes.

Swype includes a clever selection of keyboard commands that can make onscreen typing easier.

Capitalize first letter: Touch the first letter and swipe up off the top edge of the keyboard; then swipe back down to the rest of the letters, without lifting your finger.

Double letters: Use your finger to scribble on the key you want to double.

Correct mistakes or replace a word: Tap the word and then tap the correct version on the pop-up menu.

Change word to upper case: Tap the word, swipe up from the ?123 key to the shift (up arrow) key, and tap the correct version on the pop-up menu.

Display alternate characters: This is an alternative to using the shift key. If you press and hold a letter, Swype will cycle through a series of options, including the capital letter and the number that corresponds to that letter.

Cut/Copy/Paste: Press and hold the ?123 key.

Add word to your personal dictionary: Swype does this automatically as soon as you have used the word twice.

Keyboard shortcuts: These are great time savers, just like the keyboard commands in a conventional word processing program.

Select all: Swipe from the ?123 key to "a"

Copy: Swipe from the ?123 key to "c"

Cut: Swipe from the ?123 key to "x"

Paste: Swipe from the ?123 key to "v"

Insert period and space: Swipe from "." to the space bar to end a sentence

Display numerical keypad: Swipe from the ?123 key to "t"

Hide keyboard: Swipe from the ?123 key to Delete

www.: Swipe from "w" to "."

3. Using the Internet

If you have registered your Fire HD tablet, then you already have set up wireless access for it (see **Chapter 1**) through a Wi-Fi hotspot. You can manage your wireless networks from the Quick Actions Menu. Swipe downward from the top of your Fire HD screen and tap the Wireless icon to join a Wi-Fi network, switch networks, or disconnect wireless access to make your battery last longer.

Setting Up Email, Calendar, and Contacts

These three functions come as three separate apps on your Fire HD that are programmed to sync with each other. The email app needs a bit of setup work before you can sync it with the other two applications.

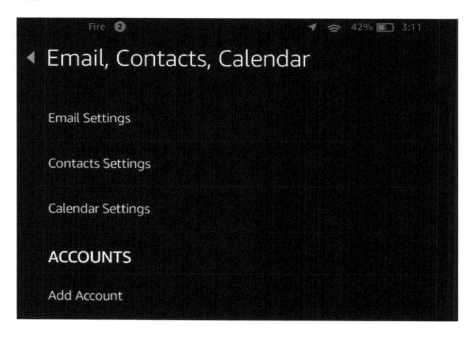

Setting Up Email: It's good to start by registering your Amazon account login email as your Fire HD's default email account, although you can start with any email account. Begin by opening the Email app. From the Home screen, tap *Apps* and then tap the *Email* icon. (You can also choose the app from your Carousel or QuickSwitch grid.) Swipe from left to right to open the sidebar menu. Tap *Settings* and then tap *Add Account*. Enter your email address using the onscreen keyboard and tap *Next*. Fill in your password and tap *Sign In*. Click *Accept* on the next screen to allow the Fire HD Email app access to your account, and wait for it to check your settings and register your email address.

Now tap *Inbox* in the sidebar menu to see your email in that account. The app will populate your Fire HD Calendar and Contacts apps at the same time. Repeat the Add Account process if you want to add your other email accounts.

The Fire HD Email app easily links with Google Gmail, Yahoo, Hotmail, and other web-hosted email services and will also import your contacts and calendar from these accounts.

Linking to email providers that the Fire tablet doesn't recognize, such as your local broadband service, or your own domain name, is a bit more involved, but we were successful on the first try by opening our email client software on our computer, opening the Accounts menu, and duplicating the settings in our Fire HD Email app. After entering your email address and password, the Fire HD Email app will ask you to choose whether to store this email as a POP3, IMAP, or Microsoft Exchange account. POP3 access downloads all of your emails to your device, while IMAP leaves them on your email provider's servers, allowing you to view all of your mail on any device you own. (Gmail also offers you the choice of accessing it as a POP3 or IMAP account, but you will need to configure this in Gmail through your web browser.)

Some users will need to set up an email account using Microsoft Exchange, especially if they need to check their workplace email account. Exchange might force you to set a password for your Fire HD lockscreen due to Microsoft's security requirements, but this is something you should do anyway (see **Chapter 2**). Once you've chosen which type of account you want to add, follow the Email app prompts to finish setting it up. Refer to your computer's email client software account settings as a guide, or use your Internet provider's support system.

Changing Your Email Settings: Once you've added your email accounts, you can change the settings by swiping from left to right to display the sidebar menu. You might need to scroll down on the sidebar to find the Settings menu. This menu lets you create separate settings for each of your email accounts, plus the Email General Settings option sets some global options for all of your accounts, such as whether to display embedded images, automatically download attachments, and include the original message in your reply.

Within individual email accounts, you can choose whether to check your email manually, or automatically at a certain time interval. You can customize each email account display name, which is what shows up in the "From" column when other people get email from you, and you can create an account-specific signature for your messages if you like. You should also name the email account you're setting up on the Fire HD so you can tell it apart from any other email accounts you set up on the device. The email applications menu also lets you specify how many messages you want your tablet to store on its internal storage drive.

The Settings menu in the sidebar also lets you add more accounts and change your default email account. You can also remove an existing email account – just remember that removing an email account also removes all stored emails, contacts, and calendars.

Using the Email App: We were pleased to find that the Fire HD email app has all the familiar functions of other email programs we have used on our desktop and laptop computers. The app looks a bit different, but the commands are the same.

When you swipe from left to right, the Email app displays a global Unread folder for all of your email accounts at the top of the sidebar menu, plus an Inbox folder and an Unread folder for each separate email account. To show more folders, choose *Show Folders* for the account you want. (Gmail accounts will say Show Labels instead, since they don't use folders.) You can tap each folder's icon to look at its contents. Tap a single message to open it and read it.

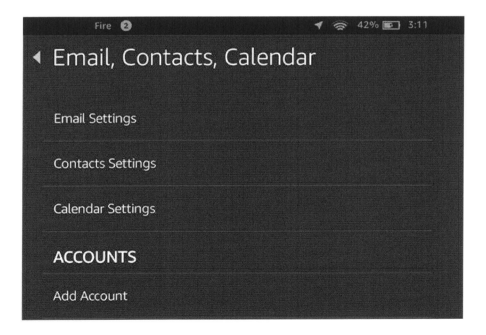

The Email app checks your messages automatically at the interval you specified in the Settings menu. To check your email manually, go to the inbox screen and swipe downward. To read a message, tap its subject line in your inbox. If you want to add the sender to your contacts, tap the sender's image in the email and tap *Add to Contacts*. You can also tap *Set as VIP* to add the sender to a separate list of VIP Contacts in the sidebar menu for quick reference.

If you want to read your messages from other devices, such as your smartphone or computer, then you might need to change some settings. IMAP accounts, such as Gmail, Yahoo and Hotmail, automatically leave your messages on their servers until you delete them. POP3 accounts are a different story – your Fire HD defaults to leaving messages on your POP3 server, but because POP3 servers don't automatically store your mail, it's a good idea to check the Incoming Settings sub menu for these email accounts to make sure!

To send a message, go to the upper-right corner of your Inbox screen and tap the "+" icon that says *New*. Type an email address in the To line. If that person is already on your list of contacts, the app will suggest an address. Now type in a subject line and type your message. Tap the *Send arrow* icon, or *Cancel* to delete.

To reply to or forward an open message, tap *Respond* and choose from *Reply*, *Reply All*, or *Forward*. Enter a To address and subject line, type your message, and tap *Send*.

To add an attachment to an outgoing email, tap the paper clip icon in the below the subject line of the email you want to send. To download or open an attachment to an email you have received, view the message, tap the *download* icon, and tap and hold the attachment to open or save it. The attachment will save to your Docs library, which you can access from the Navigation Bar.

To delete a message, press and hold the mailbox listing for any message you want to delete until a checked box appears next to it; then tap the *Delete* trash can icon.

To add a custom signature, swipe left to right to open the sidebar menu, and tap *Settings* and tap the email account you want to add a signature to. You'll then see a Signature option where you can add your personal sign-off message/signature.

> ## Top Tip!
>
> Email with lots of embedded images in them can take a lot of time to download, so if you want to make your email quicker, then go to Email General Settings (via the Quick Settings Menu) and turn off the Show Embedded Images option.

Calendar: The Fire HD Calendar app looks and acts like any other standard calendar software, but it has one extra-cool feature: it can sync with many online calendars such as Google Calendar and Yahoo Calendar. This allows you to work from the same calendar no matter which device you are using. Some Windows Live accounts are not supported by the app.

To open the Calendar app, go to the Home screen and tap *Apps*, then tap *Calendar*, or choose the app from your Carousel or QuickSwitch grid.

Contacts: This address book app syncs with your online email accounts. To open it, go to the Home screen and tap *Apps*, then tap *Contacts*, or choose the app from your Carousel or QuickSwitch grid. You can change the way the app sorts names by swiping left to right to display the sidebar menu and tapping *Contacts Settings*.

Using the Fire HD Silk Browser

Amazon's Silk browser comes pre-installed on the Fire HD. Part of this browser's functioning takes place on Amazon's own enormous servers, which work in tandem with your tablet to make your web surfing a smooth ride.

Open the browser from the Home screen by tapping *Web* at the far right of the Navigation Bar, or tap the Silk browser app from your Carousel or QuickSwitch grid.

The browser window will open with a Starter screen that displays your browsing history, labeled Most Visited sites. You can tap and hold any of the Most Visited sites to delete them from the Starter screen.

To get started with browsing, either tap to select one of the sites on the Starter screen, or type in a website URL or search term in the Search box at the top of the screen.

The layout is fairly intuitive for anyone who uses the Internet, with tabbed browsing, bookmarks, and browsing history. The only thing that initially confused us is that in the portrait position the Forward and Back arrows are at the bottom of the browser window, in the Options Bar, instead of at the top, while in landscape position the Options Bar switches them to the right.

Note that the Silk browser doesn't support Flash streaming video, but check out **Chapter 9** on troubleshooting for some possible nifty workarounds for this issue!

Basic Search: Silk combines the search box with the web address box, similar to Google Chrome. To search the web, tap the *Address/Search* box to bring up the onscreen keyboard. Type your search term into the box and tap the *Go* key at the bottom right of the keyboard to get your search results. Tap a result to open that web page. You can also type a website address directly into box, or type in a partial address and choose from the list of options that the browser brings up.

Tabbed Browsing: Tap the "+" key in the upper right corner of the browser window if you want to open a new tab to browse in. To open a link in a new tab on an existing search result or web page without leaving that page, tap and hold the link and choose *Open in New Tab* from the pop-up menu. To close a tab, tap the *X* in the right corner of the tab. To display the Starter screen when the Silk browser is already open, close each open browser tab by tapping the *X*, or tap the "+" key to open a blank tab.

Top Tip!

If it's not obvious and you want to quickly see where a particular text link on a page is pointing to, then tap and hold your finger on the link and you'll see the exact webpage address that the link will take you to.

Search Within a Page: To search a web page for a word or phrase, tap the *Menu* icon on the bottom toolbar of the browser window (look for three vertical dots). Tap *Find in Page* to bring up the onscreen keyboard and type your term into the search box. The browser will immediately highlight all instances of that term on the page. Tap *Done* to hide the search.

Bookmark a Page: Our bookmarking method of choice is to tap and hold the browser tab of the page we want to bookmark and choose *Add to Bookmarks* from the pop-up menu. The Menu icon in the Options Bar at the bottom of the browser screen also has an Add Bookmark option. To view your bookmarks, swipe from left to right to display the sidebar menu and tap *Bookmarks*. To visit a bookmarked page, tap its thumbnail. To delete a bookmark, tap the *X* to its right and tap *Delete Marked Items*.

View Your Browser History: Swipe from left to right and tap *History* to see a list of sites you have visited in the past seven days. If you want to delete your history, tap the *Clear All* button in the upper right corner of the History menu.

Personalize Your Browser: Swipe from left to right and choose *Settings* to bring up a number of customization options for the Silk browser. Most of the options will be familiar to you from other browsers, such as blocking pop-up windows, clearing the cache, and managing cookies.

We also like to use the Silk Reading View feature for web pages that support it. When you load a web page, look for the green spectacles icon that displays at the top of your screen next to the website address and tap it. Reading View makes web pages a lot easier to read. To return to normal browsing, tap the *X* in the upper right corner of the browser window, or swipe up or down.

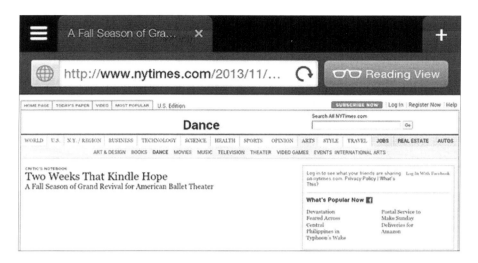

One personalization feature we use often is enlarging or reducing the browser page display magnification. There are two ways to do this. You can double tap the page to enlarge it and double tap it again to reduce it. The other method is "pinching": place two fingers on the touchscreen and spread them apart to enlarge, or pull them together to reduce. Note that you'll need to wait for the page to finish loading before either of these methods will work.

Another very cool feature we use on the Fire HD is the ability to share any web page in an email directly from the Silk Browser. Tap the *Menu* button on the bottom toolbar with the page open and tap the *Share Page* option on the menu. It's a good way to share your discoveries on the web with friends and professional contacts who don't use Twitter or Facebook.

Using Other Search Engines: The Fire HD Silk browser defaults to the Bing search engine, but if you prefer to use Google, or Yahoo, you can change the default search engine setting. Swipe from left to right, tap *Settings,* and tap *Search Engine* to choose your new default search engine.

Shopping on Your Fire HD

The Fire HD device makes shopping on Amazon incredibly easy, which is yet another smart marketing strategy for them. You can shop for digital content from within each content library on your device, or you can use the Amazon shopping app to shop the entire Amazon website at once. For digital content purchases from Amazon, you first must enable a 1-Click Payment Method in your Amazon account. (This is true even if you are downloading free content or apps.)

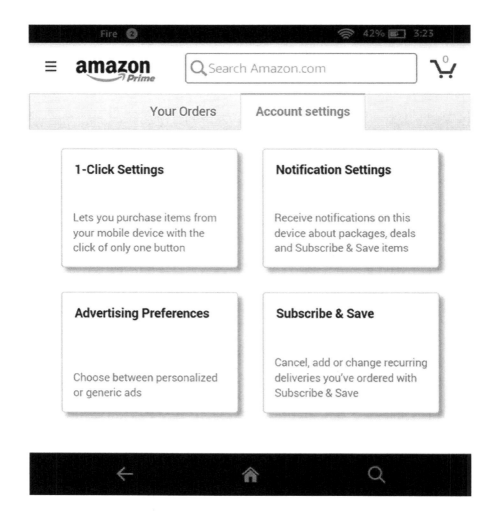

Setting Up 1-Click Payment: You will need a credit card on file with Amazon to complete this task. Open a browser window and go to Amazon's website from your Fire HD's Silk browser or a computer. Log in to your Amazon account and click the small black triangle next to Your Account under your name at the top right of the screen. Choose *Manage Your Content and Devices* from the drop-down menu and go through the additional login and password screen. Click the *Devices* tab at the top. From here you can use the *Edit Payment Method* button to add or change your 1-Click Payment options.

Shopping for Digital Content: Each of the Content Libraries on the Fire HD Home screen has its own app for accessing the Amazon store. Pick a content library, tap *Store*, and an app will open to take you on a shopping spree in that content category. For example, if you go to the Home screen, tap *Apps*, and tap *Store*, the Amazon App Store will load on your screen.

The main page of each store app will feature freebies and special sale items, with suggestions for items you might want to buy based on your past search and purchase history with Amazon.

There is an option to look at Best Sellers, and an option for New Releases. Each store's main page also includes a search box. If you already know what you want to buy, tap the *search box* to bring up the onscreen keyboard and type in the name of your item. Click the *Buy button* to purchase the item with your 1-Click Payment method and download it to your Fire tablet.

If you don't want to buy an item right away, you can tap *More Options* and tap *Add to Wishlist* so you can come back to it later. To see your Wishlist, swipe from left to right and tap *Wish List* to bring up your list.

Shopping on Amazon: There are two ways to shop on the entire Amazon site from your Kindle. The first way is to go to the Home screen and tap *Shop* in the Navigation Bar. This is the first item that appears in the toolbar, and we don't think this is any accident! The other way to shop is to tap *Apps* in the Navigation Bar and choose the *Shop Amazon* app. Either way, the user experience is very similar to shopping on Amazon from your desktop or laptop computer.

Don't Forget Amazon Prime: Your Amazon account comes with a free month of Amazon Prime (unless you've already used up this option). This opens up all kinds of free content possibilities, including the Amazon ebook lending library and Prime Instant Video, plus you get free 2-day shipping on your non-digital Amazon orders. There are special categories of Prime membership, such as student and parent, which have some restrictions on free content, so be sure to do a bit of research before you pay the fee and buy into the program.

A great feature in the Shop Amazon app is called Fling. When you see a product you want to bookmark for later, tap and hold the product image until a smaller version pops up in a square box. Drag or "fling" the smaller image into the gray circle in the lower left corner of your screen. To browse your Fling selections, tap the black circle with the three squares in the middle and tap the image for the product page you want to open. To delete a product from the Fling menu, drag its image from the menu to the gray trash can. Tap the double square icon to hide the menu.

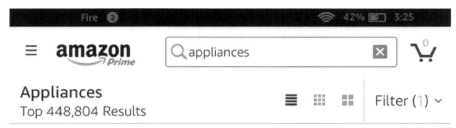

Appliances
Top 448,804 Results

Filter (1) ⌄

Lasko 754200 Ceramic Heater with Adjustable Thermostat
$24.97 $35.99 ✓Prime
Get it by Tuesday, Nov 18
64 offers from $22.97
★★★★☆ (3,615)

General Electric MWF Refrigerator Water Filter
$38.74 $62.12 ✓Prime
Get it by Tuesday, Nov 18
50 offers from $32.99
★★★★⯪ (3,501)
See more choices
#1 Best Seller in In-Refrigerator Water Filters

Green Bay Packers Infrared Helmet Heater, LW-NFL-0001
$198.99 $249.99 ✓Prime
4 offers from $198.99
★★★★★ (20)
See more choices

4. Using Apps

Applications, which we call "apps" throughout this book, are mini software programs that perform specialized tasks on your smartphone or tablet. Because they are so specific, they run lean and don't take up much room on your Fire HD's internal storage drive. There are apps for just about every task you can think of, and probably some you haven't thought of yet! Apps really are what make your Kindle fun.

The operating system on your new Fire HD 6 or HD 7 tablet is based on the Android operating system, which puts thousands of Android apps at your fingertips. Not all of them – unfortunately some Android apps just won't run on the Fire HD – but you still have thousands to choose from, and you can download them right from the Amazon App Store to your tablet. The best part is that a lot of them are free! For the inside track on some of the best apps available, check out our companion book, **250+ Best Kindle Fire HDX & HD Apps**.

The new Fire HD 6 and HD 7 tablets ship with only a few apps pre-installed. They include:

1. Silk web browser app

2. Email, Contacts, and Calendar apps

3. Shop Amazon app

Help App: This is simply a shortcut to the same App found in the Quick Actions Menu.

FreeTime: This app comes pre-installed on your Fire HD so you can use Household Profiles in the Settings menu to set up a custom selection of content for up to 4 kids. Amazon FreeTime automatically blocks access to the Silk Browser and Amazon content stores unless you authorize them. It also disables location-based services, in-app purchases, and social features unless you change the settings. No changes can be made to FreeTime without your parental controls password, so it locks your Fire HD down good and tight!

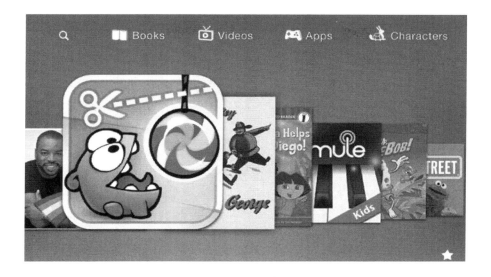

Your first step in setting up FreeTime for your child is to create a lock screen password and parental control password for your Fire tablet in the Settings menu (see **Chapter 1**). Next, create a Household Profile for your child by swiping down from the top of the screen and tap *Settings*. Tap *Household Profiles*. Tap *Add Child*, add a profile photo, enter a name, birthdate, and gender, and tap *Use Amazon FreeTime*. (You can also set a teen profile that offers many of the same security protections as FreeTime but without the custom content options. FreeTime allows you to add any content you choose to your child's profile from your Amazon Cloud Library. Tap Done to save settings and create a FreeTime profile for your child.

The FreeTime app itself is free, while FreeTime Unlimited is a monthly subscription service for the app that delivers Amazon-selected children's videos, books, educational apps, movies, and television shows. This is very smart marketing on Amazon's part – they are introducing very young users to the Fire HD in hopes of making them users for life. FreeTime content is aimed at children ages 3 through 8 and is drawn from big-name kids' media producers like Disney, Sesame Street, Nickelodeon, and even PBS, so your kids can combine learning with entertainment. The per-user price is quite reasonable, and with Amazon Prime, it's even better.

Coming Soon

A new FreeTime feature is in the works at Amazon called FreeTime Camera and Photo. It will let kids take photos and edit them to add stickers and drawings. They can then save their edited photos to their family's Amazon Cloud Library or print them for their parents to hang on the fridge or at the office.

Get Your Game On

Amazon classifies its downloadable games as apps, so they appear in two content libraries: in the app library with all kinds of other apps, and in the games library, which displays only games. To access this library, tap *Games* in the Navigation Bar. Tap *Store* to see which games Amazon is promoting on the Games page, and use the search box and on-screen keyboard to find the games of your choice. More categories of games are available when you swipe left to right to bring up the sidebar menu.

Tap the price button to purchase the game, and then tap Download to download it to your device where it will appear in both the Cloud and the On Device libraries. Like all other Fire HD apps, games must actually be stored on your device before you can use them.

Downloading Apps from Amazon

To find and download an app, go to your Fire tablet Home screen, tap *Apps* in the Navigation Bar, and tap *Store*.

Your first look at the Amazon App Store starts with the Free App of the Day. This top toolbar scrolls automatically to show app categories and special deals. In the middle of your screen you will see Featured Apps and Games, and across the bottom are Amazon's Recommended for You selections based on your browsing history. Sweep from left to right to display the sidebar menu, where you'll find even more ways to search for apps. Tap the app's icon to read its description and learn more about it.

If you're anxious to get started and don't want to read more right away, you might want to start by downloading some free apps from the App Store. Tap the magnifying glass icon at the top of the App store window to open the search box and onscreen keyboard. You can find apps like Netflix, the Weather Channel, ESPN ScoreCenter, and more, along with a number of games. Free apps are downloaded with Amazon's standard 1-Click Ordering, but your account will show a charge of $0.00. (Remember that Netflix has an "in-app purchase" meaning that it charges its own monthly subscription fee for you to use the app to stream video.)

You might notice that a banner across the App Store page says Amazon Coins. This is virtual money that Amazon manages for you so you can use it to buy...you guessed it...more apps! Amazon makes a token Coins deposit for you when you register your Fire HD, and you can purchase more Coins by swiping left to right and choosing *Amazon Coins* from the sidebar menu.

The next step is one you shouldn't skip – use the Amazon App Store search box to find and install an Android Security App on your Kindle.

Check out the **Norton Mobile Security Kindle Tablet Edition**, which screens all new data you load to your Kindle for viruses and other nasties. You also might take a look at **Lookout Mobile Security Kindle Tablet Edition**, which screens for viruses and also provides theft protection by tracing your Kindle's Location-Based Services signal. There are many other Android security apps with similar functions. Even though you will be downloading from Amazon, you should do your own due diligence.

When you find an app you want to download, it is a good idea to check out the developer's reputation by seeing if they provide their company name, and whether they are selling other apps besides this one. With an app that is advertised as free, make sure that it really is completely free or whether an additional fee is required (called an "in-app purchase") to use it. Make sure you understand the permissions you have to give this app to work on your Kindle. It seems like overkill, and we don't always do it ourselves when downloading well-known apps, but those "freebies of the day" often come out of nowhere. So trust, but verify!

To download an app, tap the price button near the description. If the app isn't free, your 1-Click Ordering account will be charged and the button will change to Get App. Free apps actually register as a sale in your 1-Click Ordering account, but the amount shows as $0.00. Tap the *Get App* button and the app will be automatically downloaded to your Kindle. When it finishes, tap the *Open* button to use it. If you don't want to use it right away, you can find it later by tapping *Apps* from the Home screen Navigation Bar to look for it. If you have downloaded or opened it recently, it also will appear in the Carousel and the QuickSwitch menu. Note that apps must be downloaded to your Kindle before you can open them, unlike the other Content Libraries on the Navigation Bar.

You can also buy Kindle apps from your PC or Mac computer's browser and have them sent directly to your Kindle. Your Amazon account will automatically detect that you have a Kindle registered and will send your download directly to your device. As soon as you power up your Kindle, or tap *Sync All Content* from the Quick Settings Menu, the app will download and open.

The Amazon App Store lists about 30 categories of apps. All these selections can be overwhelming, so we suggest that you go with a basic list at first and round out your selections later on. One good rule of thumb for downloading apps is to look at the Amazon customer reviews. Apps that average 3 stars or fewer, or have very few reviews, are probably (but not always) not as good a bet as an app with hundreds of good reviews.

Here is our favorite "must-have" list for your first visit to the Amazon App Store. All of these apps are free, although some of the developers charge subscription fees for their content.

Netflix – lets you watch movies and TV shows on your Kindle Fire when you order the in-app subscription or use your existing subscription information. If you're new to this service, downloading the free app gives you a one-month free trial.

Movies by Flixster – is the "must have" app for anyone who loves movies. Stay right up to date with new film and DVD releases, read reviews via Rotten Tomatoes and find out about local show times and even book tickets.

Songza – is like your own personal music concierge. This app offers a huge library of playlists compiled by music experts, arranged by mood, decade, type of music, and activity. And possibly best of all, unlike some other music apps, there are no listening limits or ads.

Springpad – is a really attractive way to keep notes on the move. Create as many specific notebooks as you like, access them via your Kindle or PC and never forget anything again!

AccuWeather – is the stand-out app for keeping abreast of the weather where you are. Updated every 15 minutes with an attractive interactive layout, download for free and make sure you never get caught in the rain again.

MapQuest – Since Google Maps still isn't available for Kindle, this is a popular alternative. Both Amazon and Apple are said to be pursuing their own mapping technology, so don't expect to see Google's product on your Kindle in the near future.

Angry Birds – is the most popular game app in the world, with 1.7 billion downloads. Help the colorful birds heap payback on the green pigs. Be sure to download the Kindle Tablet edition. The basic version is free, but there are numerous upgrades that aren't.

Draw Something – is an ingenious doodling game that you can play with your friends on Facebook or Twitter. The game suggests a word and gives you a set of drawing tools. When you finish, your friends have to guess the word that inspired your drawing.

Temple Run – is a game app success story with over 1 million downloads. Run your escape route from the Evil Demon Monkeys through a rich virtual landscape with hair-raising obstacles.

Where's My Water – is a Disney game app that finds Swampy the Alligator waterless when he wants to take a shower. Your job is to make your way through the city's underground water system and fix his plumbing problem.

For a whole lot more great apps, both free and paid, to suit just about every conceivable need, you can also check out our companion book, **250+ Best Kindle Fire HDX & HD Apps**.

Uninstalling Apps

If you download a lot of apps, your Fire HD's data storage will fill up quickly. It's a good idea to do a bit of housecleaning once a month or so and get rid of any apps you aren't using. Remember that any app you order from Amazon will always be available in the Cloud tab of your Amazon Cloud Library if you want to download and re-install it.

To uninstall an app, find its icon using either the Carousel, or the QuickSwitch grid. Tap and hold the icon until a pop-up menu appears. Simply tap *Remove from Device*, and the app is gone from your Fire HD but still stored safely in your Amazon Cloud library.

Once you have uninstalled an app, it won't be updated when you sync your device unless you manually re-install it. To re-install, tap *Apps* in the Navigation Bar, tap the *Cloud* tab, and tap the app's icon to download it. Apps stored on your Fire HD are visible in the *Device* tab. Be careful not to delete any paid apps from your Cloud Library, or you will have to buy them again to re-install them!

Force-Closing Apps

If an app stops working, the best solution is to just force-close it. Sweep down from the top of your screen to open the Quick Actions Menu. Tap *Settings*, tap *Applications* and then tap *Manage All Applications* to bring up a list of the apps installed on your Fire HD. Tap the icon for the stuck application and tap *Force Stop* to close it.

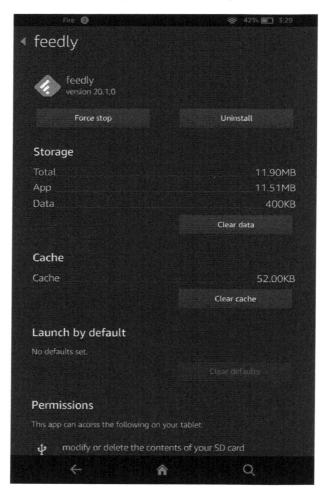

Top Tip!

Below Force Stop on each Application Details page you will also see further down the screen Clear Cache. Clicking here lets you clear your Kindle storage drive of extra data that applications sometimes generate but don't need, thus freeing up space.

Installing Third-Party Apps (Sideloading)

At first it may seem as if the selection of apps in the Amazon store is endless, but in reality, Amazon offers only a small percentage of the more than 500,000 apps available for Android. For a taste of what you're missing, take a look at the selection in the Google Play App Store **play.google.com/store/apps** and see if it seems worth your while to install apps on your Kindle from outside the Amazon App Store – a practice known as "sideloading."

This process isn't always straightforward, and some Android apps simply won't work on your Kindle, but it's worthwhile if you have a bit of tech skill or you don't mind spending some time to figure it out. Note that we're not talking about "rooting," which involves installing new firmware on your Kindle to enable the installation of third-party apps. Rooting will void your Kindle warranty and open you up to all kinds of operating problems unless you really know what you're doing.

Amazon has built a menu item for installing third-party apps on your Kindle, so it's safe to say they allow basic sideloading. Swipe down on your Home screen to display the Quick Settings Menu and tap *Settings*, then tap *Applications*. Go to Apps from *Unknown Sources* and tap *On*. This sets up your Kindle to install apps from sources outside of the Amazon App Store.

Be sure to download and install an Android Security App as described earlier in this chapter before you go any further. This is especially critical with sideloading, where an app can come from just about anywhere.

Some good places to start sideloading apps include the Opera App Store – **apps.opera.com/en_us/** (operated by the company that developed the Opera browser) and SlideMe – **slideme.org/**. Both of these sites feature Android apps for downloading and are high profile enough to reduce the risk of installing something buggy.

If you want to transfer apps from another device to your Kindle, first go to the Amazon App Store and install the **ES File Explorer** app on your Kindle. This nifty app lets you manage the stored files on your Kindle just as you would on your Mac or PC. Next, use the file explorer software on your desktop or laptop computer to transfer the app files you want from your Android phone or other device to your computer's hard drive. Look for the extension .APK, which is the Android app file extension. Then transfer the app from your computer to your Kindle, either with the mini USB cable, or as an attachment in an email to yourself (See **Chapter 8** for details of how to do this). Finally, use the ES File Explorer app to find and install each new app.

Sideloaded apps don't install and open automatically like the ones you download from the Amazon App Store. There are three different methods we use to find and open sideloads on our Kindle.

Web Downloads: Tap *Web* on the Navigation Bar in the Home screen or open the Silk browser from the Carousel or QuickSwitch menu. Swipe from left to right to display the sidebar menu. Tap the *Downloads* button and look for your sideloaded app, which should show an .APK extension. Tap it to install. If you get an error message, try *Notifications*.

View Notifications: Look in the status bar across the top of your screen for a small number in a circle just to the right of your device name. If you see one, swipe the status bar down to see your notifications.

If your sideloaded app appears in the list with the .APK extension, tap it and see if the app will install.

File Exploring App: If neither of the above options work, install the ES File Explorer app as we describe above and open it. You should see several rows of blue folders. Locate the one marked *Downloads* and tap it to see the contents. Locate the app with the .APK extension and tap it to install.

If the installation process starts, you will need to read and accept permissions for that app and wait for the installation to complete. After that, tap *Open* at the bottom of the installation screen. If all goes well, your sideloaded app will behave just like the Amazon apps on your Kindle from now on.

We have found that sideloading gets mixed results with apps that we downloaded to our Android phone from Google Play – some of them only work partially on our Kindle, and some don't work at all. But it's the closest thing to putting Android functionality on your Kindle that you can get without rooting, and we kind of like the challenge!

5. Reading Books and Newsstand Items

Amazon got its start in the book selling business, and nobody does it better. It has the largest database of book titles in the world, and the bookstore is a great place to browse and do research. Amazon's development of the Kindle as an ebook reader was another history-making event. The technology has grown so quickly that looking at our Kindle Fire HD today, it's hard to believe that the original device was a simple e-reader with a black and white screen that could only display ebooks!

Buying Books from Amazon

To shop for ebooks on Amazon, tap *Books* in the Navigation Bar on your Kindle's home screen and tap *Store*.

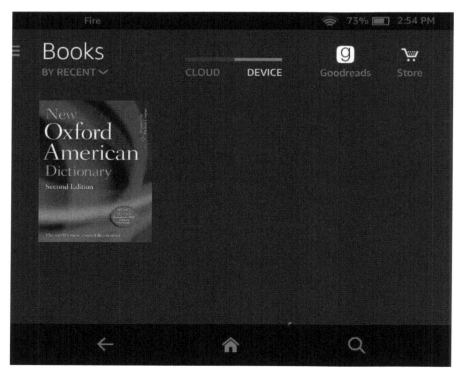

The first thing you will see in the Amazon Book Store is the Recommended for You list, which Amazon carefully puts together from your previous search and buying history. Next you will see a row of Daily Deal titles, many of which are free. Below that are the Best Sellers. Additional categories are available by swiping from left to right to display the sidebar menu. You can browse the Book Store using any of these categories. Swipe across a row of book cover displays to scroll through a list.

To learn more about a book, tap its cover. From the book's information page, you can read its description and see its Amazon reader reviews. Tapping the *Download Sample* button will download a sample excerpt to your Fire HD. Tap the *Read Now* button when the download finishes to see if it is something you want to buy.

To mark a book to look at later, tap the *More Options* button and tap *Add to Wishlist*, which will store it in your Amazon Wishlist. To see your Wishlist, swipe from left to right to display the sidebar menu and tap *Wishlist* to display the list. You may also borrow some books for free if you have an Amazon Prime membership.

To search for a certain book title, tap the magnifying glass icon at the top of any Book Store page to display the search box and type the book's title, author, or keywords into it using the Fire HD's onscreen keyboard. You can also search the book database by its ISBN number.

To buy and download a book, tap the *Buy* button near the description. Amazon will charge your 1-Click Ordering account for the price of the book and the button will change to say Downloading. If you are downloading a free title, it will still register as a sale in your 1-Click Ordering account in the amount of $0.00. When the download is complete, the button will change again to say *Read Now*. Amazon gives you the option of canceling your order if you bought the book by mistake.

You can also buy Amazon ebooks from your PC or Mac computer and send them directly to your Fire HD. Your Amazon account will automatically know that you have a Fire HD registered and will list your device in the drop-down menu marked *"Deliver to"* on the right side of your browser screen under the Buy button. Select your Fire HD from the list, and as soon as you power up your Fire HD, or tap *Sync and Check For New Items* from the Quick Actions Menu, the book will download and open.

Reading Books on Your Fire HD

Any new, unopened books on your Fire HD will appear in your Book Library with a strip across the cover that says New. You can find your newly purchased books by tapping **Books** from the Home screen Navigation Bar. If you have opened a book recently, it will appear in the Carousel as well as your Book Library. If you are in the process of reading it, the cover will display the percentage of the book you have finished so far. Tap the cover icon that appears in your Library or the Carousel to open the book and read it, or press it and hold to open it automatically. Turn the pages forward or back by tapping the screen on the right or left, or by swiping in the direction you want to move.

When you open a book to read, the Fire HD defaults to full screen mode and hides all navigation icons, which can leave you feeling stranded until you learn how to escape. Simply tap once on the book page or in the top or bottom margin. The Options Bar with the Home and Back icons will appear at the bottom, and the Reading Toolbar will appear at the top. You will also see a slider showing how much of the book you've finished. You can use the slider as a Go To command to move to a numbered location within the book. If you swipe left to right while these menus are visible, you'll bring up a full table of contents that you can tap to go to the beginning of each chapter. Tap the page again to hide these menus.

LES MISÉRABLES

VOLUME I.—FANTINE.

PREFACE

So long as there shall exist, by virtue of law and custom, decrees of damnation pronounced by society, artificially creating hells amid the

Page 1 of 959 | 1%

Managing Your Book Library: Books can really fill up your Fire HD's data storage, so Amazon gives you two tabs at the top of your Book Library screen. Titles displayed in the Cloud tab are your complete collection of book purchases, while the titles shown in the *Device* tab are the ones you have downloaded from your Amazon Cloud Library to your Fire HD device. If you want to read a book from the cloud that you haven't stored on your device, then you can only access it when your Fire HD is connected to a wireless network. This leaves more data storage space open on your Fire HD, but remember that you can't access the cloud while reading at the beach. If you plan to travel to a location with no wireless access and want to read on your Fire HD, do a bit of advance planning and download the books you want to read so they are stored on your device.

To download or remove a book from your Fire HD, find its cover using either the Carousel, or by tapping Books in the Navigation Bar. To download a book from the cloud, tap the *Cloud* tab, and tap the book's cover to download it. Books that you have downloaded to your tablet will appear with a checkmark within the cover icon. To remove a book from your device, tap the *Device* tab; then tap and hold the cover icon until a pop-up menu appears. Tapping *Remove from Device* takes the book off your Fire HD but leaves it in your Amazon Cloud Library to download again at any time. Don't delete any books from your Cloud Library, or you will have to buy them again to download them.

MatchBook: Amazon has rolled out its MatchBook feature, which offers customers a discount price on the ebook edition of any book title they initially purchased in print. Go to **www.amazon.com/ kindlematchbook** to see a list of eligible titles and a list of books you've purchased that are available in MatchBook. More titles are being added to this program all the time, so if you don't see the book you want on the list, check it again from time to time.

Kindle Reading Accessibility Features

The Fire HD ebook reader app lets you customize your reading experience from the Reading Toolbar. To display the toolbar, tap the screen while displaying any book in the reader. From here adjust the appearance of the reader screen via the options across the top. Tap *View* to customize the reader's background and text colors, enlarge or reduce the text size, change the display font, and even change the spacing. There are also some other very interesting options and functions here to choose from which can greatly improve your user experience. These include:

Text-to-Speech: For those books that are Text-to-Speech enabled, this button will let your Fire HD read text to you! To access it, go to the *View* option on the Reading Toolbar, select *More Settings* at the bottom, and then turn the *Text-to-Speech* option on.

Top Tip!

Did you know you can switch from "black on white" to "white on black" text? This can make books easier to read in the dark or if you have vision impairment. To change to "white on black" go to the Settings in the Reading Toolbar, and opt for Black in the color mode. There's a Sepia option here too that can also make text a bit easier on the eye.

X-Ray: This is a great tool for reading club fans and students. In books that are X-Ray enabled, you can use this option to find passages in a book that mention the same concept, character, places and other useful information about the book or the author. Tapping on the *X-Ray* button in the Reading Toolbar will bring up the full range of these passages for you to explore.

Share: The Share option on the Reading Toolbar is a super quick way for you to copy and share sections of a book via Twitter or Facebook.

Bookmark: Simply tap the upper right corner of the book page to create a bookmark on the page you're currently reading. Fire HD will automatically go to this page when you next open that book. To display your bookmarks, tap anywhere on the book page to bring up the Reading Toolbar and tap the Bookmarks icon on the right.

Making notes and highlighting text: Tap the screen on the first word of a section you want to highlight, then drag your finger along the section. Lift your finger and an option box will pop up asking you what you want to do with the section (either add a note, highlight or share). You can access your notes and highlights via the Notes option on the Reading Toolbar. You can also see sections of a book that other readers have highlighted by turning on the Popular Highlights option. Swipe downward from the top edge to display the Quick Actions Menu, tap *Settings*, and tap *Applications*. Tap the *Books and Newsstand* sub menu to turn *Popular Highlights* on or off.

Top Tip!

If you highlight a word or phrase and then choose More from the options, you can then search for that word or phrase either within the book, or on Wikipedia, or on the web at large! Cool!

Dictionary: The reader app also features a built-in dictionary. Tap and hold any word to bring up a quick definition. If you click Full Definition, the dictionary will expand to show you the complete entry within the dictionary. The dictionary lets you search the book for the word, search on Wikipedia, or search the web for it. You can also translate the word by typing your own language into the translate box in the corner of the definition box and selecting the language you want to translate it into – neat!

Goodreads

Amazon created yet more buzz in the book industry when it acquired Goodreads and its 20 million members. The Fire HD lets Goodreads members sync their Fire HD and Goodreads accounts to automatically post their Amazon book purchases to Goodreads. This feature allows sharing of "Want to Read" lists and rapid exchange of reading lists between Goodreads friends. To access Goodreads, tap *Books* in the navigation bar and tap the Goodreads button at the top of your library screen, or swipe left to right to display the sidebar menu and tap *Goodreads on Kindle*. You will need your Goodreads login and password information to access your account.

Downloading Free Ebooks

The Fire HD has made books more affordable than ever, and free titles are easy to find, both in the Amazon Book Store and on third-party websites. Here are some places to look for free reading material.

Amazon has two special programs that offer free books. The first is Kindle Select, which allows publishers to make their books free to build readership. Select titles are always displayed in a carousel-style menu on the home page of the Kindle Book Store, which you can scroll by swiping it. Another way to browse the Select program is from a third-party website that collects free titles. These tend to come and go on the web, but a quick Google search from the Silk browser on "free Amazon ebooks" will bring up several sites that list books in the Select program.

The second Amazon free books program is Free Popular Classics. These are older titles in the public domain whose copyright has expired. Thousands of classic works of literature are available for download to your Kindle, including Les Misérables, A Tale of Two Cities, Alice in Wonderland, and Jane Eyre. To browse this collection, type free popular classics into the search box.

Internet Archive: This nonprofit site has collected over 2.5 million book titles that you can read on your Kindle, but you will need to download each ebook to your Mac or PC first. In your computer's browser, go to **www.archive.org** and search for a title, or scroll down to browse the subcollections. Choose a book, click Details, and look in the left sidebar for the Kindle version download link. Save the file to your computer. From your hard drive, you can transfer the file to your Kindle using either the micro USB cable, or by emailing it to yourself as an attachment and downloading the book in your Fire HD's email app. See **Chapter 8** for more file transfer options.

Open Library: This enormous free library contains 1 million free ebook titles, but not all of them are available for the Fire HD, and some of them require you to register first. From your Mac or PC browser window, go to **www.openlibrary.org** and click the "1,000,000 free ebook titles" link near the top of the screen. Search for the title you want, or browse by subject, author, or keyword from the menu at the top left. Make sure you check the box that says *"Show Only Ebooks"* before you run each search. Click on a title to see whether you can download it as a MOBI file. If you can, click it to download and transfer it from your hard drive to your Fire HD as we explain above. For some titles, you can also download a Fire HD edition directly to your device from the Silk browser.

Project Gutenburg: This free site holds 30,000 titles. Use your Mac or PC to browse to gutenberg.org and search for the title you want, or browse by category. When you find a book, click the Fire HD with Images link and download it to your hard drive, then transfer it over to your Fire HD using one of the methods explained above.

ManyBooks: This library has 26,000 free ebooks. Use your computer to search for a title or browse the categories, then click on a title and use the Download menu on the right to grab the MOBI version so you can transfer it over to your Fire HD.

Borrowing Books from Amazon

Amazon is more than a bookstore – it also functions as a gigantic lending library. If you have an Amazon Prime membership, then you can borrow books for free, which really is an incredible deal. Without Prime, you will pay a fee to borrow a book. The Lending Library program limits you to one borrow per month, but there are no due dates. Only Kindle Fire and Fire HD owners are eligible for this program.

To borrow a book on your Fire HD, tap *Books* in the Navigation Bar and tap Store. Swipe left to right to display the sidebar menu and tap *Kindle Owners Lending Library* to bring up a list of titles you can borrow for free with Prime. Tap any title to display the book's information page, and tap *Borrow for Free*. The book will download to your Kindle and open for you to read. You can add notes and highlights to a borrowed book just as you can for a book you own, and they will be saved in your account.

The easiest way to return a book is simply to borrow another one. During the borrowing process, Amazon will prompt you to return the old one. Another method is to go to the Amazon home page in the Silk browser and choose *Manage Your Content and Devices* from the drop-down menu under *Your Account*. Tap the *Actions* button next to the title you want to return and follow the prompts.

Borrowing Amazon Books Through Your Local Library: Amazon's Overdrive program allows more than 10,000 libraries in the United States to lend Amazon ebook titles to their patrons who have Amazon accounts – no Prime membership required! Each library has its own lending policy, but generally there are restrictions on how many ebooks you can borrow at a time, and how long you can check them out. You will also need to set up an account and PIN for the library you are using.

From your Fire HD's Silk browser or your laptop or desktop computer, use your library's online card catalog to search for ebooks (some libraries call them digital books). Click on the title and click *"Get Ebook"* or a similar-sounding link. At this point you will need to select your library name and type in your PIN number. The book and its description will appear in a new screen. Click the ***Borrow*** button and choose Kindle format from the drop-down menu. Overdrive will now take you to the Amazon website. Click the ***Get Library Book*** button on the right and download it to your Fire HD or your computer. If you used your computer for this, you will need to transfer the book's MOBI file to your Fire tablet using the instructions above or in **Chapter 8.**

If the Borrow button has been replaced with a ***Place a Hold*** button, then you will have to place a hold on the title to read it later – Amazon Overdrive limits the number of copies of any single title that can be checked out in your library system at one time. Unfortunately, if your title is checked out, you will have to backtrack several screens to search for another one, and possibly enter your PIN again.

The advice above is one way to go. Another option is to download and use the **Overdrive Media Console** app which you can download for free from the Amazon app store (use the link or just search for "Overdrive"). Using this app should allow you to do everything necessary to complete the whole process from one place. We haven't used this app and have heard mixed feedback with some Fire tablet users absolutely loving it and other saying that they can't get it to work. Looking at recent reviews suggests that improvement and fixes have been made.

Lending Your Fire HD Books to a Friend: You can lend items from your Book Library to one person for up to 14 days. The borrower can read it on a Kindle Fire or Fire HD, or on a PC or Mac after downloading and installing the Kindle Reader software. To lend a book, go to the Amazon home page in the Fire HD Silk browser or your computer browser, and choose ***Manage Your Content and Devices*** from the drop-down menu under **Your Account** and go to the ***Content*** tab. Tap the ***Actions*** button next to the title you want to lend and choose ***Lend This Book***. Amazon will prompt you for the borrower's password. Click the ***Send Now*** button. Note that lending is not available for some Amazon titles, and that each of your books can only be loaned once. You will not be able to read the book while it is out on loan.

Buying and Reading Newsstand Items

The Newsstand is where you can subscribe to magazines, newspapers, and blogs that require a subscription fee. Amazon is promoting the newsstand by offering all magazine subscriptions in the Newsstand free for the first 30 days. Tap *Newsstand* in the Navigation Bar and tap *Store*. You will see a carousel of magazines, with selected promotions across the top, another carousel of Most Popular magazines that offer their first issue free, and below that a carousel of categories. Swipe across your screen to scroll any of these carousels. To start a subscription through 1-Click Ordering, tap any item and tap the *Try Free for 30 Days* button, or the *Buy Issue* button. Note that the free 30 day subscriptions will automatically renew unless you cancel them from your account page under *Manage Content and Devices*. Also, these free Newsstand items with interactive features will require a free app for that item, which you can download from the App Store and then activate your subscription with an in-app purchase.

To view your Newsstand items, tap *Newsstand* in the Navigation Bar. Your 30 days free promotional items will appear in the Carousel. The Fire HD only keeps the current issue of each Newsstand item on your device. To see up to 12 back issues of any magazine or 14 back issues of any newspaper, tap the title in your Newsstand Cloud tab and tap the back issue you want to download to your Fire HD.

Older back issues can be downloaded from your Subscription Settings page. You can access this page a couple of different ways. The easiest way is to swipe down from the top to open the Quick Actions menu, tap *Settings*, tap *Amazon Account Settings*, and tap *Subscriptions*. Sign in and use the *Actions* button to deliver past issues to your Fire HD. If you have purchased a Newsstand item with a free 30-day trial, you can cancel your subscription from this page before Amazon charges your credit card for it.

You can also use the Silk browser or your computer browser to navigate from Amazon's home page to your Amazon account page and finally to your Manage Your Content and Devices page. Using the Content tab, you can download back issues and activate or cancel subscriptions to newsstand items using the Actions button on the right.

Top Tip!

If you prefer, you can also save individual articles from magazines, rather than saving the whole issue. All you have to do is access the article as usual, then tap on the 'Menu' icon and select the 'Clip This Article' option. The article will be saved in your Newsstand, even if the rest of the magazine gets deleted!

6. Listening to Music

Your All-New Fire HD 7" makes a great music player, and its sound system is a major improvement over the first Fire release. The Fire HD features Dolby sound output and a hefty pair of speakers built into the back of the case. We were surprised to find that holding the Kindle doesn't interfere with the sound quality, nor does a properly designed protective case made specifically for the HD (see **Chapter 10**). You can make your Kindle sound even better with a good pair of headphones (see **Chapter 10**).

Buying Music from Amazon

To shop for music on Amazon, tap *Music* in the Navigation Bar on your Kindle's home screen and tap *Store*.

The Amazon Music Store features a carousel of promotions, a Songs Recommended for You list, an Albums Recommended for You list, and a Featured New Albums list. Additional categories are visible when you swipe left to right to display the sidebar menu. You can browse the Music Store using any of these categories. Swipe across any row of thumbnails to scroll through a list, or tap any thumbnail to learn more about the selection. From the selection's information page, you can tap the arrow within the icon for any track to listen to a sample clip.

To search for an album or song, tap the magnifying glass icon to display the search box at the top of any Music Store page and type an album, song, or artist into it using the Fire HD's onscreen keyboard.

To buy and download a selection, tap the *price* button, which will change to say *Buy*. Tapping it again will charge your 1-Click Ordering account for the price of the selection and store it in your Music Library. Free downloads still register as a sale in your 1-Click Ordering account in the amount of $0.00. A pop-up menu will open and give you the choice of either going to your Music Library and listening to your purchase, or continuing to shop.

Prime Music: Amazon has sweetened the deal for its Prime members by offering them a huge catalog of albums, songs, and pre-selected Prime Playlists absolutely free. You can also create your own playlists by mixing up Prime Music selections with your own musical tracks and saving the result.

If you're a Prime member, you can browse for Prime Music selections in the Amazon Music Store by tapping *Music* in the Navigation Bar and swiping left to right to display the sidebar menu. Tap *Prime Music* and scroll down to see Amazon's selection of free songs in the Prime Music catalog. If you tap *See More* you'll see a lot more songs to choose from. Simply tap the blue *Add* button to add the song to your Amazon Music Library in the cloud. You can also use the search box on any page in your Music Library to hunt for your favorite song, artist, album, or genre, tap *All Genres* in the top left corner. Tap *Filter* on the results screen and choose *Prime Music Only*. You can also pick out Prime Music selections while browsing the full music library by looking for a selection with the diagonal Prime banner across its icon.

Any Prime Music selections you add to your Music Library display right along with your other songs and albums, no matter how you sort the items (by album, song, artist, or genre). The Prime Playlists section under "Your Playlists" shows the Prime Playlists you've added to your library.

Prime members can listen to their Prime Music selections in their Music Library in the cloud on virtually any device they own, as well as directly on Amazon.com. Prime Music can only be downloaded to phones and tablets that support Amazon Music. This app is built into your Fire HD, but you must download it to other devices, and your Prime Music selections can't be exported to other devices. You must access your downloaded selections while connected to a wireless network every 30 days or it is automatically deleted.

Be aware that Prime Music titles come and go, so if Amazon decides to remove a selection from Prime, you will need to purchase it before you can listen to it again.

AutoRip: Like many music lovers, we still buy music CDs from Amazon. We like the album art and liner notes, and their sound quality is better than MP3 files, but of course you can't play them on a tablet or smartphone without ripping them to MP3 format first. That why we love Amazon's new AutoRip service. As soon as your CD order ships, AutoRip automatically puts an MP3 copy into your Amazon Music Library, where you can listen to it from the Cloud tab, or download it to your Fire HD and play it from the *Device* tab. Not only that, it automatically adds all of your Amazon CD purchases dating back to 1998 to your Music Library – awesome!

There's only one catch: some of your CDs might not be eligible for this service, depending on their copyright terms – boo!

Listening to Music

To listen to music on your Fire HD, tap *Music* from the Home screen Navigation Bar and scroll through your library to find an album or song. If you have opened a selection recently, it will appear in the Carousel as well as your Music Library. Tap any thumbnail to open and play a selection. You can also select a playlist by tapping its name. (We explain how to create playlists later in this chapter.) When you play a song from an album or playlist, your Fire HD will move to the next song when the first one finishes. The player controls will display whenever a song is playing. Tap on the appropriate button to pause, skip to the next or previous song, shuffle, or repeat. You can use the slider here to adjust volume, or use the manual volume controls located on the side of your Fire HD.

Amazon has rolled out a song lyrics feature for selected songs in its music store. As you play one of these songs on your Fire HD, you will see the lyrics displayed on your screen and scroll line by line as the song progresses. Photos and facts about the artist are featured along with song lyrics. More and more songs are becoming available with this feature.

Listening from your Amazon Cloud Library: Your Fire HD contains a built-in media player for streaming music through your Fire HD from your Amazon Cloud Drive data storage account. (See end of **Chapter 1** for more about the cloud.) Your Fire HD's internal data storage isn't big enough to hold an extensive music library, but your Music Library in the cloud contains your complete collection of Amazon music purchases, plus you can buy additional storage space in your Amazon Cloud Library account to add music you didn't purchase from Amazon to your Music Library.

We have found that it's more convenient to store our music in the cloud and stream it, even though it uses somewhat more battery life. To stream music stored in your Music Library, tap *Music* from the Home screen Navigation Bar. You will see a tab labeled Cloud and a tab labeled Device at the top of the display. Tap *Cloud* and tap a thumbnail to play an album, playlist, or song. Cloud selections are added to your Carousel as you play them, just like any other media.

Listening Offline: If you are traveling to a location with no Wi-Fi access, then storing as much music as you can fit on your device will be a better option. In your Music Library, tap the *Device* tab to the right of the Cloud tab. This will display only the music stored on your device, where you can choose the selections you want to listen to.

To download music from the cloud, open your Music Library from the Navigation Bar, tap *Cloud*, find your selection on the list, tap its thumbnail, and tap *Download*. To remove a selection from your Fire HD, tap and hold its title in your Device library until a pop-up menu appears. Tapping *Remove from Device* takes it off your Fire HD but leaves it in your cloud Music Library to download again at any time. Remember don't delete any music from your Music Library in the cloud, or you will have to buy it again to download it!

Top Tip!

The Kindle Fire comes with an (albeit limited) Equalizer so you can customize your listening experience to suite your taste. To access the Equalizer, go to the Settings and choose 'Enable Equalizer Modes' to then see a selection of modes and options to explore.

Managing Your Music Library

Sorting Your Library List View: You can sort the items in your Music Library by swiping left to right to display the sidebar menu. Sort features include your choice of album, song, artist, playlist, genres, and other labels. Tapping the *List View* or *Grid View* arrow in the in the top left corner of your Fire HD screen lets you toggle your Music Library between List View or Grid View. The search icon in the Options Bar is handy for finding selections.

Creating Playlists: Your Music Library creates separate playlists for the Cloud and Device tabs. You will need a Wi-Fi connection to create a cloud playlist. To create a playlist, go to your music library, tap and hold the icon for the song or album you want to save, tap *Add to Playlist* from the pop-up menu, and tap *Create New Playlist*. Then use the onscreen keyboard to give it a name and tap *Save*. To delete an item from a playlist, swipe left to right to display your playlists, tap and hold the icon for the playlist you want to edit, tap *Edit*, and tap the "-" symbol next to the song.

Prime Playlists: If you're an Amazon Prime member, check out the selection of pre-populated playlists available in your Music Library. From the Navigation Bar on the Home screen tap *Music* and swipe left to right to display the sidebar menu. Tap *Prime Playlists* to bring up compilations like "Pop to Make You Feel Better" and "Singing in the Shower," as well as more conventional classic rock and techno lists. Lengths vary from 90 minutes to over 3 hours so you can tap a list and forget about it while it plays. Playlists are sortable by category or genre by tapping *All Playlists* in the top right corner of your Music Library display.

Transferring Your Music to the Cloud

Amazon Music gives every customer free storage in the Amazon Cloud Library for 250 songs not purchased from Amazon in addition to unlimited free space for all Amazon purchases. You can upgrade your Amazon Music account to import up to 250,000 songs for $24.99/year. Amazon Digital Music purchases do not count towards these limits. For us it was a no-brainer to buy more space in our Amazon Cloud Library to make our entire music collection available on our Fire HD. We like the peace of mind of storing a copy of our entire music collection in a safe place, too.

To import your personal music collection to Amazon Music, go to your music library at https://www.amazon.com/musiclibrary from a web browser on the computer you want to import your music from. Click *Import Your Music* and follow the prompts to install the Amazon Music Importer. The Importer searches your iTunes and Windows Media Player libraries, or you may manually choose the folders where your personal music collection is stored. Choose which songs to upload, or click *Import All.*

The importer will read most music file formats, but you will have to copy your CDs to your computer's hard drive before you can upload them. Third-party music ripper software makes this quick and easy. It's best to set the output format to MP3 to save time and to free up space on your computer's hard drive.

Buying and Listening to Audiobooks

Audiobooks have their own library that you can access from the Navigation Bar on the Home screen of your Fire HD. Tap *Store* to shop for audiobooks on Amazon. Shopping for and managing this library is very similar to buying and managing ebooks from your Books Library (see **Chapter 5**). The Audiobooks shopping menu has a Wishlist option, and it downloads your purchases automatically through your 1-Click Shopping account. Titles are added to the Carousel on your home screen if you have recently downloaded or opened them, and you can call up a list of your audiobooks from the Navigation Bar. You can leave your audiobooks in your Amazon Cloud Library, or download them to your Fire HD, but keep in mind that audiobooks take up a lot of storage space on your device. Like all of your Fire HD's content libraries, you can tap the *Cloud* tab to display all of your audiobook titles, or tap the *Device* tab to see only the ones stored on your device.

The Fire HD's built-in audiobook player displays a control panel where you can adjust its reading speed to slower or faster than normal, add bookmarks, pause the audio, back up 30 seconds, and adjust the playback volume. The player control panel also has a Sleep function that we really love. You can actually set your Fire HD to read you to sleep at night for 15 to 60 minutes, or to the end of a chapter – lovely!

You can add a note when you place a bookmark by tapping and holding the *Bookmark* key until the onscreen keyboard pops up. To display your list of bookmarks, tap the small notebook icon in the upper right corner while the audiobook is open in the player. Tap and hold any bookmark to edit your notes or delete the bookmark. Swiping left to right will display the sidebar menu with lots of options for managing your audiobook library and player. The sidebar menu also contains options for jumping from chapter to chapter and details about each audiobook title.

Although Amazon audiobooks aren't part of the Lending Library program for Prime members, we found that our local library loans out selected audiobook titles through Amazon's Overdrive program (see **Chapter 5**).

Audible App: This Android app is free to download from the Amazon App Store and offers some great features if you opt for the monthly subscription plan as an in-app purchase. Audible is an Amazon company, so their website sells the entire library of Amazon ebooks and audiobooks for you to read or listen to on your Fire HD. You can purchase your Audible subscription from the Amazon App store or from your Mac or PC. The cheapest plan gives you one free audiobook per month plus discounts on additional audiobook purchases, while the expanded plans cost more but give you more free audiobook downloads. We listen to a lot of audiobooks, and they aren't cheap to purchase, so this subscription plan has been worthwhile for us.

Check out Audible's Immersion Reading feature, which highlights each word of your audiobook in the text version as the word is spoken. Audible also manages Amazon's Whispersync function, which saves the highlights and bookmarks you place in your Fire HD ebook library and syncs them across all of your devices.

And you can also set the Audible app to be Button-Free – opening your user experience to a more fluid interaction with the use of some neat shortcuts. For example, once your book is playing through the Audible app, you need only tap anywhere on the Fire HD screen to pause or play, swipe left or right to go backwards and forwards, swipe down to skip a chapter, and tap and hold the screen to create a bookmark.

7. Watching Movies

With its HD resolution display and excellent audio quality, the All-New Fire HD 7" might be the ultimate portable video player. Amazon's video store has over 150,000 titles, and the Fire HD's small size lets you take your movie watching anywhere you go. However, for the time being, Amazon's Instant Video Service is only available in the United States, the UK and Germany.

Amazon has also developed its exclusive Advance Streaming and Prediction (ASAP) technology to address a common customer complaint about Internet video streaming: buffering. You've probably experienced stuttering, "hanging", and audio out of sync with the video when you play videos through your computer's web browser, and possibly with other digital media players you've tried out. Buffering occurs because most people's broadband service isn't up to the heavy bandwidth usage demands of digital media streaming. Amazon's solution is to tap into your user history and use it to predict which movies and TV episodes you might want to watch. These titles are preloaded into your account on their server. If you buy or rent one of these titles, they're already buffered for you and waiting for instant playback A-S-A-P.

Buying or Renting Videos from Amazon

To shop in the Amazon Instant Video store, tap *Videos* in the Navigation Bar on your Fire HD's home screen and tap *Store*.

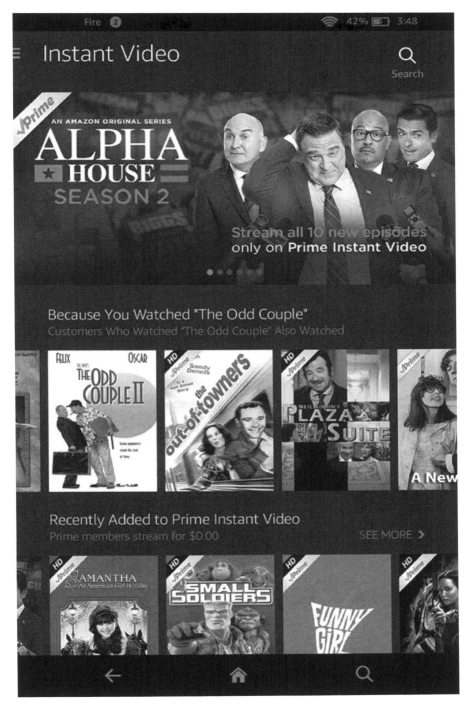

The top half of the store is devoted to Amazon's Prime Instant Video service. All of the videos in this category are also available without a Prime membership – they just cost more! The lower half of your screen displays Amazon's suggested videos for you based on your viewing history, recently added to Prime Instant Video, and top picks.

To search for a video, tap the search box at the top of any Video Store page and type a title or set of keywords using the onscreen keyboard. To delete your video search history, tap *Videos* in the Navigation Bar on the home screen and swipe left to right to display the sidebar menu. Select *Settings*, and then tap *Clear Video Search History*.

To use the X-Ray feature to learn more about a video, tap its thumbnail in the Video Store to see a rich selection of facts and trivia from the Internet Movie Database (IMDb), which is also available for free as an app in the Amazon App Store.

Most Video Store movies will have a *Watch Trailer* button under the thumbnail so you can see the preview. TV shows will list which seasons are available and their prices.

Swipe from left to right to display the sidebar menu, where you will find your Watchlist. You can add videos you have purchased and videos you want to save for possible purchase later to this list. To scroll through the Watchlist, swipe down the display of thumbnails. To mark a video in the Store to return to later, tap the *Add to Watchlist* button for that item.

For each video in the store, the *Buy* and *Rent* Buttons appear on the right side of your screen with a price shown for each. If no Rent button appears, then the video is not available for rental. Clicking one of these buttons will charge your 1-Click Ordering account so you can get the video. You can choose to start watching it right away, or save it in your Video Library.

Renting Videos: If you tap the *Rent* button, 1-Click Ordering immediately charges you for the rental. The rental period for videos is only 24 hours, but it doesn't begin until you actually start to watch the video. Be sure to select whether you want to rent the HD or SD version during the rental process. There is no need to return a rental video – it simply becomes unavailable when you tap it in your Video Library or Carousel until you rent it again or buy it. We think that this alone is a good reason to rent your videos on Amazon!

Amazon Prime Instant Video: Thousands of videos in the Amazon store are available to Prime members for free – yes, you read that right! All Prime Instant freebies can be streamed to your Fire HD through your Wi-Fi connection, and Amazon now over half of this collection for downloading as well. This really is an incredible deal and is just one more excellent reason to buy a Prime membership.

Watching Videos

By default, all of your purchases from the Amazon Video Store are streamed to you via your Wi-Fi connection to save data storage space on your Fire HD. Streaming requires you to be in an area with an active Wi-Fi connection, and remember that it uses up some battery juice on your device. To watch a video, tap the item in your Video Library, in the Carousel, or in your Watchlist and then tap *Watch Now*. To go back to a video you haven't finished, tap its thumbnail in your Video Library screen.

Video Player Controls: To display the video player control panel, simply tap the screen while you are watching a video. The slider allows you to turn the volume up or down. The pause button lets you pause or resume the video when you tap it. There is also a 10-second skipback button to rewind the video 10 seconds. Finally, the video scrub bar lets you move forward or backward in slow motion through the video to a frame of your choice by dragging your finger across the bar.

Watching Downloaded Videos: If you want to watch a video in a location with no Wi-Fi connection, then you will need to download it to your Fire HD first. Tap the video's thumbnail in your Video Library, the Carousel, or the Watchlist and tap *Download* to save the video to your Fire HD. The menu will give you the choice of downloading the video in HD or SD format, and your answer will depend on how much storage space is left on your device and how important HD resolution is to you for this particular video. If you want to pause or cancel the download, tap the *Options* button. To view the downloaded video from your Fire HD without a Wi-Fi connection, tap the video's thumbnail and then tap *Watch Now*. Remember that some Prime Instant Video selections are not available for download.

Top Tip!

If your Wi-Fi video streaming goes all juddery, then it could be due to a weak Wi-Fi signal. Try turning off any other downloads you might be doing at the same time or, failing that, download the video to your Kindle first and then watch it.

Managing Your Video Library

You can choose whether to view a downloaded video through Wi-Fi streaming or from your device by using the Cloud and Device tabs in your Video Library. Tap *Videos* from the Home screen Navigation Bar. At the top of the Video Library display you will see a tab labeled Cloud and a tab labeled Device. Tap *Cloud* to select a streaming video. Switch to the *Device* tab to display only your downloaded videos.

Videos are displayed in your library in the order you downloaded them.

Streaming from Third-Party Sites

Third-party video streaming services like Netflix and Hulu Plus are battling it out with Amazon for the biggest share of the video market. For the moment, Amazon seems to be winning, but if you want to try out these services, you should start by downloading their free apps from the Amazon App Store (see **Chapter 4**). Both services charge a monthly subscription fee as an in-app purchase.

Free video streaming sites such as YouTube and Vimeo have one issue with the Fire HD, and that is the Silk browser's lack of support for Flash video, but in **Chapter 9** you'll see that we've found some possible workarounds for this issue.

Watch Movies on Your TV

The Fire HD 6 and HD 7 tablets offer two ways to watch Amazon Instant Video on your HDTV.

Second Screen: Amazon's Second Screen feature lets you stream any Amazon Instant Video through your wi-fi network from your Fire HD 6 or HD 7 to your Amazon Fire TV, PlayStation 3 or 4, or a 2013 Samsung Smart TV. Using Miracast technology you can fling movies and TV shows from your tablet to a big screen while using your Fire HD tablet as a remote to control playback and other functions. You can even browse the web, check your email, or use Amazon's X-Ray feature to learn more about the movie you're watching.

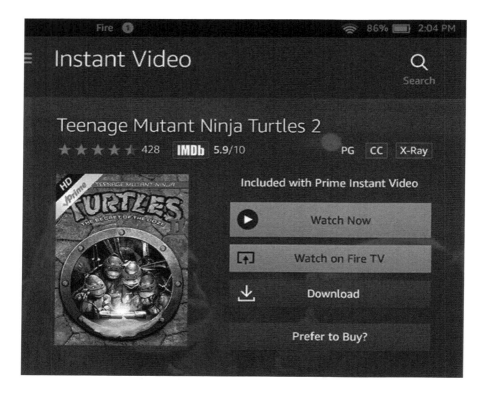

To activate Second Screen, tap Videos from the Navigation Bar, choose a video from your Video Library or the Amazon Store, and tap its thumbnail. Make sure your Fire HD is within wireless range of the compatible device where you want to watch. To start the video, tap Watch Now for Prime Instant Video, or Buy or Rent your selection from Amazon Instant Video. When the video starts, tap the Second Screen icon ⬆ on the bottom right of the video player control panel. Your Fire TV, PlayStation, or Smart TV will now display your video until you tap the Second Screen icon again and tap Fire tablet to exit Second Screen mode.

If you're using other apps on your Fire tablet while watching a video on Second Screen and you want to switch the video back to your tablet, tap Videos again from the Navigation Bar. Swipe left to right to display the sidebar menu, tap the name of your selection, and tap the Second Screen icon. Note that Second Screen doesn't support viewing on your Fire HD and your big-screen device at the same time.

Second Screen also lets you stream photos you store in your Amazon Cloud Library to a compatible big-screen device for gatherings with friends and family.

Display Mirroring: This is only available on the Fire HD 6 and HD 7 if you purchase an HDMI dongle like the Fire TV Stick or Google Chromecast. Plug the dongle into the HDMI port of any HDTV and follow the instructions for setting it up. On your Fire HD tablet, swipe down from the top and tap Settings, then tap Display & Sounds, then tap Display Mirroring. Choose your display device and tap Connect. Your HDTV will now display whatever appears on your Fire tablet screen.

8. Working with Photos and Documents

With their front-facing and rear-facing cameras, the Fire HD 6 and HD 7 tablets have joined the ranks of bona fide tablets such as the far more expensive Apple and Samsung products. You can now take photos, videos, and self-portraits, and the built-in microphone makes Skype calls and video chat a reality.

Taking Photos with the Fire HD Tablet

To use the Fire HD tablet's built-in cameras, tap the Camera app in the carousel or QuickSwitch menu, or you can access it by tapping Photos in the Navigation Bar on the Home screen and tapping the camera icon. When the app opens, tap the double arrow icon to toggle back and forth between the two cameras on your tablet. The front-facing camera faces toward you, while the rear-facing camera faces away from you.

To take a photo, tap the shutter icon. Your image will be automatically saved, but Image Review briefly displays the image so you can delete it if you wish by tapping the *X*.

To turn *Image Review* on or off, tap the gear icon to display the *Camera Settings* menu and use the toggle slider to activate or deactivate it. This menu also allows you to activate or deactivate *HDR* (High Dynamic Range) for the rear-facing camera only, which will give you better photo quality in low light or shadowy settings. Tap the gear icon again to hide the camera settings.

To exit the Camera app and return to your Photo Library screen, tap the *back arrow* in the Options Bar. The Share icon in the Photo Library lets you share the image via email, Facebook, or Twitter. The edit icon offers some nice editing features for retouching and optimizing your photos right on your Fire tablet.

To enable storing your photos in your Amazon Cloud Library, activate Auto-Save from the settings menu. Swipe left to right, scroll down and tap *Settings*, and turn *Auto-Save* on or off.

The Photos Settings screen also shows your total Cloud Drive usage. If you tap *Manage*, the Fire HD will exit the Photo Library screen and open the Amazon Cloud Drive login screen in the Silk browser. Note that photos taken with your Fire tablet don't count against your storage limit in your Cloud Library.

Taking Videos: The rear-facing camera records videos with sound. Open the Camera app and tap the red video icon to start recording. You can zoom in and out by pinching the screen with two fingers, or by using the volume buttons on the edge of your tablet's case. Tap the video icon again to stop recording and store or delete the video.

Taking Panoramic Photos: The rear-facing camera takes long photos in either a horizontal or vertical direction. Activate the Camera app from the Carousel or from Photos in the Navigation bar. Open the Camera app and tap the gear icon , then tap *Panorama*. Tap the blue capture icon and move your Fire tablet slowly in the direction you would like to capture the panoramic photo, or touch and slide the arrow in the preview strip. Tap the white square inside the blue capture icon to save.

Using Skype with the Fire HD

Skype is a free app that lets you chat with other Skype users all over the world for free with video chat, voice chat, and instant messaging. With its front-facing camera and built-in microphone, the Fire HD is a good friend when you want to Skype.

If your Fire HD didn't come with the Skype app pre-installed, tap *Apps* from the Navigation Bar and use the search box to find it in the Amazon App Store. Download it and open it. If you're already a Skype user, log in with your user name and password, or register an account if you're a newcomer to Skype.

Before you start chatting, set up your profile by tapping the head and shoulders icon in the upper right corner of the Skype home page. From this menu you can upload a profile photo or avatar by tapping the larger head and shoulders icon that pops up. *Choose from gallery* lets you upload any photo from your Fire HD Photo Library, while *Take photo* activates the tablet's Camera app so you can take a self-portrait and upload it. The profile menu also lets you choose whether to let your contacts know you're available, or keep your status invisible. Either way, your contacts can still call you.

The icon to the right of your profile icon with the three vertical dots displays the *Skype Settings* menu. Here you can control how you sign in, receive notifications, and manage privacy functions. If you don't want to see Microsoft targeted ads, uncheck that box.

It's time to add some contacts. Tap the *Add Contacts* icon (the head and shoulders with the + sign) at the top of the screen and search the Skype director for people you know who use Skype. When you find someone you'd like to Skype with, tap *Add to Contacts*. This will send your contact a message requesting permission to be added to your Skype contacts. If they say yes, you'll be ready to chat.

To chat on Skype, go to your list of contacts and tap the name of the person you want to call. To voice chat, tap the telephone receiver icon below their name; to video chat, tap the video camera icon. You'll hear a ring tone until they answer the call. If you're doing a video chat, be sure to hold your Fire HD with the front-facing camera pointing toward you. For instant messaging, tap the + icon at the bottom center of the screen and type your message in the box, then tap the arrow icon to send the message.

As you use Skype, you'll see items like Skype Wi-Fi and Skype Credit, which involve spending money. Skype Wi-Fi creates a wireless hotspot for you to use Skype in areas where no wi-fi connection is available, and Skype Calling lets you dial cell phone and land line numbers from your Fire HD tablet. Both of these services cost money, but as long as you don't add funds to your Skype Credit account with a credit card, Skype will automatically limit you to its free services.

Transferring Photo and Document Files

For transferring an occasional photo or document file between your Fire HD and another device, an attachment sent through your regular email account works fine. For sharing photo albums and other multiple file collections, you will need something more heavy duty. Here are three ways to transfer data between other devices and your Fire HD.

USB Transfer: To transfer files between your Fire HD and a computer, plug the full-size end of the micro USB cable into a USB 2.0 port on your computer, and plug the micro end of the cable into your Fire HD. (Mac users should install Android's free File Transfer app on their computer first, from **www.android.com/filetransfer/**). Once connected, your Fire HD will display as an external drive icon in your computer's file directory. Click it open, then click the Internal Storage folder, and then the Documents folder to display the files on your Fire HD's storage drive.

On your computer's hard drive, find the file you want to transfer and simply drag and drop it to the Fire HD's Documents folder. Eject the Fire HD device icon from your desktop before unplugging the USB cable. The Fire HD should automatically detect the type of file you have transferred and will put it in the correct content library. When you open that library, the transferred file will show up under the Device tab. It won't show up in the Cloud tab because the Fire HD doesn't back up USB transfers to the cloud.

You can also drag and drop files from your Fire HD to your computer's hard drive with a USB connection. These files can then be transferred to another Kindle Fire or Fire HD, or to a smartphone.

Personal Documents Service: This Amazon service lets you send multiple files and large files between your Fire HD and another device. Unlike a USB transfer, this method stores your data files safely in the cloud where you can retrieve them at any time. There is no charge to use this service over Wi-Fi.

Your Fire HD assigns you a unique email address for using the Personal Documents Service. To find it, tap Docs at the far right of the Navigation Bar on your Home screen and tap the *Email* icon. Look for an email address that ends with @kindle.com and jot it down.

Before anyone can send documents to your Amazon email address, you need to pre-approve their email address. Go to your Amazon account via your PC and choose *Manage Your Content and Devices*, then click the *Settings* tab at the right and scroll down to *Personal Document Settings*. You can then enter the sender's address under Approved Personal Document E-mail List by clicking *Add a New Approved Email Address*. You should also add any of your own email accounts that you plan to use for this service.

Approved senders can send you up to 25 attached documents per email, with the size of each document limited to 50MB before zipping. You must receive and open the email with the Fire HD email app within 60 days to avoid deletion. Personal Documents Service will store the attachments in your Amazon Cloud Library, where you can download them to your Fire HD at any time by tapping *Docs* in the Navigation Bar and viewing them in the *Cloud* tab. Download a single file by tapping its icon, or download multiple files by tapping the *Select* icon in the upper right corner of the Docs screen and checking the boxes next to the documents you want to download.

You or another sender can speed up the document attachment process on their end by downloading and installing the Send to Kindle application to their computer or Android device. Amazon makes versions of Send to Kindle for PCs, Macs, Android, and specific web browsers. Go to **www.amazon.com/sendtokindle** to download it for your device.

For really heavy-duty uploading, you can install the Amazon Cloud Drive desktop application on your computer and upload up to 2GB of data at a time directly to your Amazon Cloud Library account, where it's available for viewing or downloading in the Cloud tab of your Kindle libraries.

To install Cloud Drive on your computer, go to **www.amazon.com/gp/drive/app-download** and let the site automatically detect which version you need before it presents you with a download. You can also click *Your Cloud Drive* from the drop-down menu under Your Account on the Amazon home screen and install the application from there. Open and install the downloaded file to your hard drive. This application will then let you connect to your Amazon Cloud Library with your computer so you can upload and download data with a simple drag-and-drop interface.

Alternatively you can just upload your documents, photos and videos straight into your Cloud Drive account via your browser. Go to the main **Amazon Cloud Drive page** and instead of clicking on 'Install Cloud Drive' click on *Your Cloud Drive* located at the top right of the page. Once there you will see a series of content folders and by clicking upload you can browse your computer for the relevant content you wish to store.

Working with Documents

Office Suite: The WPS Mobile Office for Amazon app on your Fire HD has the same functionality of Microsoft Office on your Fire HD. Tap *Docs* in the Navigation bar to open your Document Library and the + symbol labeled *New*. You'll be able to create and save files formatted as Word documents, Excel spreadsheets, and PowerPoint presentations. This app also edits documents created in Office and uploaded to your Amazon Cloud Library, transferred to your Fire HD via USB cable, or sent to an email account. The WPS app also creates a PDF of Word and Excel documents to save or print to a wireless printer.

Wireless Printing: The Fire HD has a robust wireless printing option. From the WPS Office app, your Photo Library, or the Fire HD email app you can send documents, spreadsheets, emails, images, and presentations to any printer connected to a wi-fi network. The Fire HD auto-detects all available printers in your network.

Business Productivity: The Fire HD can be set up to log in to your company's intranet, even if it's set up with Microsoft Exchange. You can the great selection of office productivity apps for the Fire HD to submit timesheets, expense reports, share and edit documents, and sync your email, contacts, and calendar. Remote VPN access with full encryption is also available from the Settings menu for even greater connectivity and security.

Creating Folders

We like the free **ES File Explorer** app for creating and managing folders on our Fire tablet. This nifty little app gives your tablet's storage drive full Windows-like functionality. You can create new folders, select multiple files or folders, drag and drop files and folders, rename them, and – if you dare – delete them. The app also creates shortcuts and has a really well devised search function that sorts by name, date, file size, or category. To install it on your Fire HD, tap *Apps* in the Navigation Bar to go to the App store and use the search box to find it and download it.

Other Useful Image/Document Functions

Sending PDFs: In order to send a PDF document, you will first need to convert it to the AZW format for the Fire HD. But this is simplicity itself as your Fire tablet has a built in converter tool – all you have to do is type the word "convert" into your email's subject line, then attach the PDF and send the message to your Amazon email address (see above).

Taking Screenshots: To capture a screenshot from your Fire HD at any time, place your fingers on the outside edge of your device and press and hold the Power button and the volume-down part of the Volume button at the same time. If you press them both at the exact same time, your Fire tablet will make a shutter clicking sound, fire off a screenshot and save it in your Photos content library. To go to the album, tap *Photos* in the Navigation Bar.

Saving web images: Tap and hold the web image and an options box will pop up; simply choose *Save Image* and the image will be saved onto your Fire HD.

Sending multiple images: First tap *Photos* in the Navigation Bar, and tap the sharing icon in the upper right corner next to the trash can icon. You will be prompted to select all the images you want to send by tapping on each image. Finally tap the *Email* button to attach all of them to your email. If you want to send a single image, simply tap and hold it, then choose Email from the list of options. You can also use this screen to share your images on Twitter and Facebook.

Changing your Fire HD wallpaper: For the ultimate customization, you can use your own images as the wallpaper of your tablet. To do this, first download the free **Rotating Wallpaper app**. This is not an Amazon app so you will need to be comfortable with sideloading apps and search for the app online (see **Chapter 4**). Once you have it open the app and click on the *Add Set* option.

You will be asked to name the new set and then prompted to add pictures to the set from your Fire tablet. Finally, choose the timing, orientation and order of the images from the app settings for a truly personal look for your tablet. Note that if you don't want to use your own images or can't get the Rotating Wallpaper app, there are many other good wallpaper apps available to download – we quite like the free **Cool Wallpapers HD app** which has an absolutely huge, and constantly updated, gallery of images to choose from.

Coming Soon

Amazon is planning a new feature called Family Library that will allow family members to link separate accounts and share their digital content with one another without logging in and out of multiple accounts. Shareable items will include apps, games, audiobooks, books, and Prime Instant Video content.

9. Troubleshooting

What to Do if Your Fire HD Tablet Freezes

If your Fire HD touchscreen completely freezes so you can't force-quit a troublesome app (see **Chapter 4**), then it's time for a hard reset. This should be done without the 5W adapter or USB cable plugged into the device. Press and hold the Power button for 20 seconds before releasing it, then restart.

If you still experience problems, you can try charging the battery through the USB cable and adapter, unplug, and then do another hard reset followed by a restart.

If a hard reset doesn't solve the problem, go to **http://www.amazon. com/customer-help** on your computer for support.

Managing Fire HD Updates

It's worth remembering that once you've downloaded an app or ebook, you usually have also allowed the developer to send you updated versions. Updates often allow for smoother running of an app, or improved content. These updates are usually automatic and show up in your notifications but from time to time, you might also want to manually check for any updates via the **Manage Your Fire HD website**. If there are any updates available for either your apps or books you should see a notification next to the title of the product.

Preserving Battery Life

There are a number of useful steps you can take to help conserve the battery life of your Fire HD, some of which will really depend on how you use your it (see our list below). But almost everyone should consider doing the following as a matter of course.

Firstly, when you're not using your Fire HD, but don't necessarily want to turn it completely off, you should use the Sleep Mode option to avoid using up battery power. To activate Sleep Mode, press the *Power button* for a couple of seconds: the Fire HD screen should go black immediately without offering up any command options. If you press the Power button for too long, a message will pop up asking you if you want to shut down – press *Cancel* if the answer is no! To "wake up" your Fire HD, simply press the *Power button* again.

You can also choose to set your Fire HD so that it automatically goes to Sleep Mode after a certain time period of inactivity. Go to Settings from the Quick Actions Menu, then choose *Display & Sounds*; here tap on the *Display Sleep* option to choose the time delay you want before the Fire HD goes into Sleep Mode.

Secondly, you can make sure that apps you're not using are not actually still running – sometimes apps don't fully switch off. Check to see which ones are still running by tapping *Settings* from the Quick Actions menu and then *Applications*. Click *Manage All Applications* and tap each app on the list to see its status. An app that has the Force Stop button grayed out is not running, but if isn't grayed out, you can tap it to force quit the app. You can also clear the app's cache by tapping the *Clear Cache button*, or you can *Clear Data* if the application is "seriously misbehaving" (as the pop-up window describes it) and you want to revert to a clean installation of the app. Clear Data does not delete the app from your device. Use the *Uninstall* button if all else fails, since the app will still be available in your Amazon Cloud Library.

Also from Manage All Applications, you can choose which apps you definitely want to run as soon as you turn on your Fire HD by choosing the *Automatically Launch by Default* option. At the bottom of each app's management screen you'll see the app's permissions on your Fire HD. Some of these can be quite intrusive, while others prevent your Fire from sleeping so you'll have to charge your battery more often. It's a good idea to know what your apps are doing while you're asleep!

Some other things you can do to prolong the Fire HD's battery charge include:

1. Using headphones to listen to audio instead of the speakers

2. Turning down screen brightness

3. Turning off the Automatic Brightness option

4. Disabling Wi-Fi and Bluetooth when you aren't using them

5. Avoiding weak Wi-Fi signals as the Fire HD has to work harder to stay connected

6. Disabling Location-Based Services in the Settings. (This function will occasionally serve a pop-up menu telling you that an app or website is looking for your location. Just tap cancel to make it go away.)

7. Checking for email messages less often

8. Opting for Airplane Mode – but remember that this will mean disabling online access

Top Tip!

And to keep your Kindle and its battery in optimum condition, make sure to avoid using it or storing it in places that are too hot or too cold. Ideally, the Kindle works best in ambient temperatures (no lower than 32 and no higher than 95 degrees Fahrenheit).

Forgotten Password

Losing your password or parental controls password means you will have to reset your Fire HD to its factory defaults. This will wipe out your registration and all data stored on the device. If you have transferred data through the USB cable, that data will not be stored in the cloud and will be lost.

Swipe down from the top of the screen to display the Quick Actions Menu. Tap *Settings* and then tap *Device*. Tap *Reset to Factory Defaults* and tap the key confirming that you really want to do this. When the reset is complete, restart your Fire HD and go through the registration process again (see **Chapter 1**).

You can also use Reset Factory Defaults to empty the storage drive and delete your Amazon account registration before selling or giving away the device.

Displaying Flash Content on the Fire HD Fire

The Silk browser on the Fire HD 6 and HD 7 tablets has an Experimental Viewer to support Flash video. To enable it in the Silk browser, swipe left to right and tap *Settings* in the sidebar menu. Scroll down and check *Prompt for Experimental Streaming Viewer*. When you find a Flash video online that prompts for the viewer, simply tap the orange *"Yes, Start Streaming"* icon to watch the video.

If you can't get a video to play in the Experimental Viewer, hardcore Fire HD users report that their favorite work-around, which has also worked well for us, is to use the **ES File Explorer app** to enable sideloading (see **Chapter 4**) and then sideload the **Dolphin HD browser** and **Flash Player APK** files. Both of these can be found by following the respective links above. After downloading them or transferring them from another device, use the File Explorer to find them on your Fire HD storage drive. Tap the files to install them, starting with Dolphin and then Flash Player.

YouTube is moving away from the Flash format, so we've had good results watching YouTube videos on our Fire HD – the secret is to tap that big black square that shows up on the video page. Rotate your Fire HD to the landscape position and you'll find that the video quality is surprisingly good.

Troubleshooting Wi-Fi Connections

Wi-Fi connection problems can interfere with data transfers and video streaming, or they can cut you off completely. Sometimes they occur if you don't enter the correct password, or if the network is running MAC filtering. MAC-filtered networks require the network administrator to manually add you as a user before you can use their Wi-Fi connection.

A bad Wi-Fi network connection can also be caused by too many users at once, or connectivity problems from the Fire HD side. Try putting your device to sleep while the power is on by briefly touching the Power button and touching it again to wake it up. You will need to slide the lock button on the touchscreen and enter your password. This process stops and starts the network connection. If this doesn't work, try restarting your Fire HD.

We have found that different types of Wi-Fi networks work better with the Fire HD than others. If you just can't connect, try using your computer's Wi-Fi utility to see whether your network is a WPA2 type as we've found that it's the friendliest for connecting to your Fire HD.

Traveling Overseas with Your Fire HD

The most important thing to be aware of when traveling outside the United States with your Fire HD is that many other countries use 220 volt electrical current instead of the 110 volt used in the US. Be sure to purchase a specialized power adapter or quick charger to handle this.

You will want to travel with your adapter and USB cable, because you probably won't have access to a computer with a USB connection long enough to handle the longer charging times.

Wi-Fi access can be sporadic overseas, so plan to download all the content you will need onto your Fire HD's storage drive before you leave home.

Extended Warranties

Your new Fire HD 6 or HD 7 tablet comes with a one-year warranty as a standard feature. If you tap Shop in the Navigation Bar and go to the Kindle store on the Amazon website, you can find some extended warranty options for the Fire HD serviced by third-party providers. A typical plan provides coverage for 2 years against things like accidents and mechanical or electrical failure. Check whether the warranty includes sending you a replacement Fire HD immediately after you make a claim, with no deductible or shipping fee, and whether the warranty is transferable.

Where to Go for More Help

The Fire HD Help Home Page is located at **www.amazon.com/ kindlesupport**. From here you can access one-on-one tech support via phone, e-mail, or chat. The Help page also contains a nice set of support documents for your All-New Fire HD 7". The Help app that comes pre-loaded on your Fire HD is a tablet-friendly version of these features.

Several Kindle Fire and Fire HD forums are available on the web that you can access from your browser. Don't believe everything you read in Internet forums, but sometimes they contain hidden gems for troubleshooting your Fire HD that you can't find anywhere else. Here are some forums that we have found helpful:

1. **Amazon Customer Forums**

2. **Kindle Boards**

3. **Mobile Read**

And also be sure to verify that the advice you are reading is specific to the new Fire HD 6 or HD 7 device, because most of the support pages for the earlier Kindle Fire models or the Kindle Fire HDX don't apply to the new Fire HD 6 and HD 7 tablets.

10. Fire HD Accessories

Another thing that makes the Fire HD so much fun to own is the huge selection of accessories for it. Some of them are must-have items, and some of them are nice-to-have items, but all of them make your experience of owning a Fire HD just a little bit better. To shop for accessories, start in the Kindle Store on Amazon.

Cases, Stands, Skins and Screen Protectors

A nice case for your Fire HD is one of the first things you should buy after you purchase the device itself. We prefer a folio-style case that feels like a book when you hold it in your hands. Remember that the case should specifically say that it fits the new Fire HD 6 or HD 7, because cases for the Kindle Fire HDs are not interchangeable. Look for a microfiber lining and a secure closure for the case cover so it doesn't accidentally come open. Another good feature is a set of grooves so you can use the case as a stand to make watching videos more comfortable. Be sure to pick a case that doesn't muffle the speakers on the rear of the Fire HD. Don't forget to pick out a color and fabric you like. Leather cases cost a bit more, but they do look sharp!

If you choose a case that doesn't double as a stand, you can buy a separate stand for video watching. Stands come in a number of designs, including folding travel stands, rigid stands, and stands with adjustable angles.

Lately skins have become all the rage for personalizing your smartphones and tablets. They are essentially a kind of sticker that you attach to your Fire HD – usually an easy enough process provided you follow the directions that come with the skins. You can buy all kinds of different skin designs for your Fire HD and there are even websites offering design-your-own custom skins. Make sure that any skin you purchase is compatible with your Fire HD's specs, and please be aware that these skins are purely decorative and do not provide any protective function at all!

The Kindle Store also sells several types of touchscreen covers for the Fire HD. You can buy inexpensive adhesive plastic film, or a more substantial anti-glare cover to fit over the screen. A good screen protector will keep your Fire HD's touchscreen from getting scratched without blocking your touch commands.

A quick search of the Amazon Kindle Store will turn up some nice stylus touch pens to make your swiping and tapping easier. People with big fingers will be especially happy with these! Now that we have a stylus, we use it all the time.

Car seat tablet holders and mounts

An item which may be of interest to parents, are the different tablet holders designed to attach to the driver or front passenger seats to hold a tablet so that passengers on the back seats can watch whatever you've downloaded onto it. Essentially, it is a clever alternative if your car doesn't have a built-in DVD player and seat screen system – and for some parents it is a lifesaver for those long holiday road trips! In a similar vein, you can also purchase tablet mounts that attach your tablet to the front dashboard area – useful to operate GPS systems or view a pre-downloaded map. With either of these items, double check that they fit the specs of both your car and your new Fire HD 6 or HD 7 tablet!

Chargers and Adapters

Amazon took the hint from numerous user reviews after the release of the 2012 Kindle Fire HD, which didn't include a charger. The new Fire HD 6 and HD 7 tablets ship with a 5W adapter to use as a charging device along with a standard USB cable. The adapter charges the Fire HD in less than 4 hours from 0% to 100% by plugging it into a wall outlet and connecting it to your Fire HD with the USB cable. The adapter can provide your tablet with continuous AC power, but we have found that it's not very convenient to use our Fire HD with it tethered to a wall plug!

Another handy power source to have on hand is a car charger that plugs into your vehicle's 12-volt power supply. These often come bundled in a kit with a case and other accessories.

External Devices

The Fire HD packs a lot of hardware value into its small size, but you can make it even more valuable by plugging in an external device. We list some of the most popular ones below.

Fire Keyboard: This external Bluetooth keyboard is incredibly thin and light so it can go wherever you and your Fire HD. Don't let its compact size fool you – it has great features, like a built-in trackpad and shortcut keys to frequently performed tasks like checking email and playing music and videos. It even has an Instant Search feature. The Fire Keyboard works with all Fire HD models.

Headphones: Although the Fire HD's built-in speakers sound pretty good, a pair of high-end headphones can deliver sound quality good enough to satisfy music lovers, and even a cheap pair of earbuds will keep you from distracting the people around you when you're listening to music or watching videos. The headphone jack is located on the same edge as the power switch of your Fire HD.

Bluetooth Devices: The Fire HD's Bluetooth capability allows it to connect wirelessly to a number of external Bluetooth devices. You can purchase headphones, earpieces, microphones, headsets, and external keyboards with Bluetooth capability.

These devices will turn your Kindle into something very much like a desktop computer, without a jumble of messy cords and cables.

To set up a Bluetooth connection between your Fire HD and a wireless device, called "pairing," you need to turn on the external device first and make sure it is within range. Consult your owner's manual for the external device and find out how to set it to pairing mode. Next, pick up your Fire HD and swipe down from the top of the screen to open the Quick Actions Menu. Tap the *Wireless* icon and then tap *Bluetooth*. Tap the *On* button next to enable Bluetooth. Look at the Available Devices menu to see if the Fire HD has detected the Bluetooth signal from the external device. Tap the device name to connect it to your Fire HD. There might be additional prompts or pairing instructions before the two devices can start "talking" to each other.

The Status Bar at the top of your screen will show the "B" Bluetooth icon when Bluetooth is turned on. Remember that turning off Bluetooth will extend the length of time between battery charges on your Fire HD.

A Final Reminder About Updates

So you got this far, and we hope you found the book useful – we just want to leave you with a reminder about the FREE Fire HD app updates for this book. If you want to take advantage of this, **sign up for the updates here: www.Lyntons.com/updates**.

Don't worry, we hate spam as much as you do so we will never share your details with anyone.

And Finally...

So there you are, you should now have all the tips, tricks and user information you need to get the most out of your new Fire HD 6 or HD 7 tablet. We are confident that we have covered all the information you could need, but we are only human so if you think we have missed anything important, or could have explained something better, we would love to hear from you. In fact we'd love to hear any comments you have about our book – you can contact us here: **BestKindleApps@gmail.com**.

All feedback will be treated in strictest confidence and we will be more than happy to make improvements for our next edition where we can.

Just before we go we would like to ask for your help. As we're sure you know, book reviews on Amazon play a huge part in helping people choose what they should be reading – and it's one of the ways that small independent publishers, like us, can get our voices heard.

So if you've found our book helpful we'd love it if you could take a minute to leave us a review. Thank you for reading.

Made in the USA
Middletown, DE
06 May 2015